Covenantal Dispensationalism

An Examination of the Similarities and Differences Between Covenant Theology and Dispensationalism

Matthew Stamper

WestBow
P R E S S

WestBow Press books may be ordered through
booksellers or by contacting:

WestBow Press
A Division of Thomas Nelson
1663 Liberty Drive
Bloomington, IN 47403
www.westbowpress.com
1-(866) 928-1240

ISBN: 978-1-4497-0112-3 (sc)
ISBN: 978-1-4497-0113-0 (e)

Library of Congress Control Number: 2010924406

Printed in the United States of America

WestBow Press rev. date:3/15/2010

DEDICATION

This work is dedicated to my wonderful children, Taylor and MacKenzie. I love you both so much and thank my God for both of you daily.

ACKNOWLEDGEMENTS

Without the patience and support of my wife Maggie, I would never have brought this work to completion. Many times I did not believe I could complete such a task, but she encouraged me to see it through. We are one flesh, and this is as much a result of her efforts as it is mine. She helped by taking care of our home, clearing my schedule so that I would have time to research, and she is and has been my best friend and number one fan through this process. I could not have done this without her.

This work considers issues it otherwise would not have if not for the debates, dialogues, and discussions I had with so many wonderful Christian thinkers and friends. Especially during this time Chad Ashman, Dr. Terry Wilder, Kevin Pomeroy, Chad Scruggs, and Trevis Smith were representative of friends I engaged with multiple times to gain perspective. I also want to thank Dr. Stephen Carlson, who encouraged me to continue my education, and provided the original idea for this work. I cannot express how much his mentoring and encouragement inspired me to produce the following work.

I would also like to thank my father, Dr. James C. Stamper, who reviewed the entire work for me and made many helpful suggestions that have helped bring this work into a more readable form. Any mistakes, errors, and omissions that remain are of my own creation.

TABLE OF CONTENTS

INTRODUCTION

Does Dispensationalism really teach that people in the Old Testament were saved by obedience to the Law instead of faith in God? Is Israel the focus of the Bible instead of Jesus Christ according to those who are adherents of the hermeneutical school known as Dispensationalism? Does Covenant Theology teach that the Church has replaced Israel? Does Covenant Theology teach that the promises God made to Israel are supposed to be understood as applicable now to the Church? Questions abound concerning the true teaching of Dispensationalism and Covenant Theology. Misunderstandings and mischaracterizations of each hermeneutical school take place when opponents fail to take an objective look at what the other school actually believes and teaches. For example, John Gerstner spoke of Dispensationalism in a way many current Covenantal theologians speak and interact with Dispensationalism:

> "What is indisputably, absolutely, and uncompromisingly essential to the Christian religion is its doctrine of salvation... If Dispensationalism has actually departed from the only way of salvation that the Christian religion teaches, then we must say it has departed from Christianity. No matter how many other important truths it proclaims, it cannot be called Christian if it empties Christianity of its essential message. We define a cult as a religion that claims to be Christian while emptying Christianity of that which is essential to it. If Dispensationalism does this, then Dispensationalism is a cult and not a branch of the Christian Church. It is as serious

as that. It is impossible to exaggerate the gravity of the situation."[1]

The word "cult" has many negative connotations, and evangelicals are all too familiar with the term to miss the importance of such an accusation, even if such an accusation is qualified with a multitude of "if" language. Gerstner, a professor of Church history and a well-respected theologian in his own right, however, should have known that Dispensationalism no more teaches more than one way of salvation than Covenant Theology does. If Dispensationalism or Covenant Theology did have as a core belief such a teaching, the system should rightly be discarded. But the truth is that neither Dispensationalism nor Covenant Theology teaches that multiple plans of salvation have taken place throughout the history of Israel. The example given highlights the common mischaracterization one side displays to the other.

On the other end of the theological and hermeneutical spectrum, generally in opposition to Dispensationalism, stands Covenant Theology. Covenant Theology is a system of interpretation and way of interpreting the Bible that is often offered up as an alternative to Dispensationalism. It offers a more simplified view of the overall unity of the Bible; typically breaking down the dispensations contained therein to two. One dispensation consists of a period of time where perfect obedience to all of God's commands, or obedience to His one command, is the responsibility and is placed upon one individual. The span of this covenant is roughly three chapters in Genesis. The other covenant is in effect until Christ returns, where the same set of standards are in place, but one person is able to fulfill the stipulations on

---

1   John H. Gerstner, *Wrongly Dividing the Word of Truth: A Critique of Dispensationalism* (Brentwood, TN: Wolgemuth & Hyatt, 1991), 150.

behalf of all who have failed. This covenant is not automatic, but is predicated on belief. This gracious covenant, known as the Covenant of Grace, is soteriological in its nature. By deduction, the former covenant with Adam is shown to be soteriological as well, even though no one is to face eternal judgment on the basis of this Covenant of Works, including Adam. Therefore Covenant Theology is presented as a simpler way to understand God's salvific plan than Dispensationalism. It is here, where Dispensationalism is understood as an intricately designed, overly cumbersome series of charts and graphs that overcomplicates the Bible, that Covenant theologians have the greatest challenge following the Dispensationalist position. Dispensationalism is not a series of scenes between God and man where different requirements are exacted that, if followed correctly, will lead to salvation. Dispensationalism is merely a system used to help interpret the Bible, not a series of soteriological situations where man is expected to play by a certain set of rules to receive salvation.

Often these two hermeneutical schools are considered to be mutually exclusive. They are deemed incompatible with one another and therefore a theologian must be to some degree one or the other. Any attempt to harmonize the two is seen as fruitless. Because of this, most theologians find themselves choosing between the two, and this in turn leads to the respective adherents of each system spending a lot of time and energy refuting the opposition instead of learning from each system those things that endear the system to biblical truth.

A risk that Dispensationalists run by lumping Covenant Theology as a whole into the category of "bad theology" or worse, "heresy," is that they may miss the depth and richness of God's grace as displayed throughout biblical history to a certain degree in a unified fashion. The Covenant of Grace reveals a truth about the eternal plan of God to redeem His chosen people. An accurate picture of God's salvific plans may be incomplete if the Dispensational student loses the forest for the trees by slicing and dicing the Scriptures into multiple dispensations without regard to the unity that permeates all of Scripture. However, God unfurled His great plan of salvation over a period of years and through multiple dispensations. Within the pages of Scripture are found significant differences between the dispensations and differences between the covenants that God has entered into with man, and this should caution any person considering a dismissal of Dispensationalism in favor of Covenant Theology on the basis of complexity. As simple as the gospel is to understand, the depths of the Bible could be mined for a lifetime and still not exhaust the innumerable truths about God found therein.

A stronghold of Dispensationalism has been Dallas Theological Seminary. Almost the entire movement of Progressive Dispensationalism can be traced to the faculty of the school.[2] In the doctrinal statement a mention of Covenant Theology (esp. the Covenant of Grace) can be located:

Article V—THE DISPENSATIONS

> We believe that the dispensations are stewardships by which God administers His purpose on the earth through man under varying responsibilities. We believe that the changes in the dispensational

---

2   Craig Blaising and Darrell Bock, *Progressive Dispensationalism* (Wheaton, IL: BridgePoint, 1993). Although Blaising is a Vice-President with Southwestern Baptist Theological Seminary at the time of this publishing, he has worked with Bock and others in the field of study. For a detailed treatment of the current trends in Progressive Dispensationalism, see the works of the faculty at Dallas Theological Seminary.

dealings of God with man depend on changed conditions or situations in which man is successively found with relation to God, and that these changes are the result of the failures of man and the judgments of God. We believe that different administrative responsibilities of this character are manifest in the biblical record that they span the entire history of mankind, and that each ends in the failure of man under the respective test and in an ensuing judgment from God. We believe that three of these dispensations or rules of life are the subject of extended revelation in the Scriptures, viz., the dispensation of the Mosaic Law, the present Dispensation of Grace, and the future dispensation of the Millennial Kingdom. We believe that these are distinct and are not to be intermingled or confused, as they are chronologically successive.

We believe that the dispensations are not ways of salvation nor different methods of administering the so-called Covenant of Grace. They are not in themselves dependent on covenant relationships but are ways of life and responsibility to God which test the submission of man to His revealed will during a particular time. We believe that if man does trust in his own efforts to gain the favor of God or salvation under any dispensational test, because of inherent sin his failure to satisfy fully the just requirements of God is inevitable and his condemnation sure.
We believe that according to the "eternal purpose" of God (Eph. 3:11) salvation in the divine reckoning is always "by grace through faith," and rests upon the basis of the shed blood of Christ. We believe that God has always been gracious, regardless of

the ruling dispensation, but that man has not at all times been under an administration or stewardship of grace as is true in the present dispensation (1 Cor. 9:17; Eph. 3:2; 3:9, asv; Col. 1:25; 1 Tim. 1:4, asv).

We believe that it has always been true that "without faith it is impossible to please" God (Heb. 11:6), and that the principle of faith was prevalent in the lives of all the Old Testament saints. However, we believe that it was historically impossible that they should have had as the conscious object of their faith the incarnate, crucified Son, the Lamb of God (John 1:29), and that it is evident that they did not comprehend as we do that the sacrifices depicted the person and work of Christ. We believe also that they did not understand the redemptive significance of the prophecies or types concerning the sufferings of Christ (1 Pet. 1:10–12); therefore, we believe that their faith toward God was manifested in other ways as is shown by the long record in Hebrews 11:1–40. We believe further that their faith thus manifested was counted unto them for righteousness (cf. Rom. 4:3 with Gen. 15:6; Rom. 4:5–8; Heb. 11:7).[3]

Buried in this wonderful exposition of Dispensationalism is a charge that Dispensationalism and Covenant Theology are incompatible: "We believe that the dispensations are not ways of salvation nor different methods of administering the so-called Covenant of Grace. They are not in themselves dependent on covenant relationships but are ways of life and responsibility to God which test the submission of man

---

3   Doctrinal Statement – Dallas Theological Seminary, http://www. dts.edu/about/doctrinalstatement/ (accessed 09/23/2009).

to His revealed will during a particular time." One of the goals of this work is to see if such a statement is adequate. Could such a statement concerning the Covenant of Grace be accurate and yet not denigrate God's gracious act in saving sinners that has been in effect since the Garden?

Dispensationalists, including those at Dallas Theological Seminary, are very clear that there has only ever been one way of salvation. But a lack of true comprehension of the Covenant of Grace, because of its unbiblical trappings of Replacement Theology and infant baptism, sometimes bring about wholesale rejection of Covenant Theology by Dispensationalists. This work additionally seeks to curb these misunderstandings that Dispensationalists have towards Covenant Theology.

Unfortunately, it is not just the theology of both schools that are caught in the crossfire. Dispensationalists are often dismissed from theological debate a priori, as though anyone who claims to be a Dispensationalist is immediately labeled unscholarly, foolish, and a frequenter of Bible conferences.[4] Covenant theologians are sometimes considered overly allegorical papists.

The truth is that both sides have representatives within their theological camp that tend to obfuscate and muddy the waters when it comes to understanding what the Bible teaches and then applying that teaching within the grid that filters the hermeneutic adopted by the school. The major components of each method of hermeneutics need to be scrubbed to see if the biblical record agrees with the doctrines taught by the respective methods. Through the past few centuries, both views have claimed within their camp brilliant men and women of faith who truly love the Lord and desire to follow whatever the Bible does in

---

4   Paul S. Karleen, *The Handbook to Bible Study: With a Guide to the Scofield Study System* (New York: Oxford University Press, 1987).

fact teach. So how do such good intentioned people come to such disparate views of God's relationship with His Creation? Is there no point of contact, no common ground on which Dispensationalists and Covenantalists agree? The reason that a need exists for such a project as this is that the divide between Covenant Theology and Dispensationalism has only deepened over time. The tenets of one system have been increasingly understood as completely incompatible with the other as confessions and statements of faith have been based on the ever-maturing teachings and formulations of the systems. Therefore the hypothesis of this work is: *Is Covenant Theology truly incompatible with the teachings of Dispensationalism? Could there be room at the "theological table" for a hybrid approach to these systems? Is Covenantal Dispensationalism a valid "new" hermeneutical school embracing the biblical aspects of both systems while rejecting the unbiblical aspects?*

The largest obstacle to unity, and perhaps the key to unlocking such a unity, is in bringing to light the objectives that each hermeneutical system sets out to achieve and to determine if the biblical record provides positive evidence to support these goals. Even if Covenantalists falsely accuse Dispensationalists of believing in multiple ways of salvation, the truth is that both systems understand that God's glory is made manifest as He redeems sinners.

If a new view of the dispensations and covenants can be seen from the light of the eternal promise of God found in Genesis 3:15 and carried forward throughout Scripture, perhaps a modification can be made to congeal with the biblical teaching concerning the promises of God. The promise of salvation is found first in the biblical record in Genesis:

> Genesis 3:15 has been called the *protevangelium*, the first Gospel. This first Messianic prophecy comes

in a most unlikely place—in the context of a curse upon Serpent. The verses assure Serpent that he would have a battle on three different levels.

1. On the personal level the woman would do battle with Serpent. She would never again be the pushover she had been in the garden. God promised to put enmity in her heart toward Serpent. This was the beginning of the successful struggle against Satan. Needless to say, God did not force this enmity upon the woman. He was responding to her sense of shame and free admission of guilt. How was this a punishment for Satan? The woman's enmity toward Satan smashed his dreams of recruiting all mankind for his rebellion against God.

2. The battle would continue between the seed of woman and the seed of Serpent. That the word "seed" here is figurative is obvious from the fact that women do not literally have seed. The seed of woman would embrace all those who share the woman's enmity toward the Devil, i.e., righteous mankind. The seed of the Devil would include all who yield to the Evil One without so much as a skirmish, i.e., wicked mankind. God was assuring Serpent that a righteous remnant of mankind would resist with God-given might the evil designs of the children of the Devil.

3. The struggle between the two seeds would reach its climax in a confrontation between Serpent himself and a single representative of the seed of woman. Serpent will strike at the heel of this champion of righteousness. He will thereby inflict great pain

upon him. Ultimately, however, the representative of the seed of woman would crush Serpent's head, i.e., deal him a mortal blow. That Genesis 3:15 refers to the victory of Messiah over Satan is the teaching of Galatians 4:4–5 and 3:15ff.[5]

Arguably, this *protevangelium* is the first evidence of the gospel which unites the entire Bible together. Goldsworthy says of this:

> Genesis 3:15 is sometimes referred to as the *protevangelium*, the first hint of the gospel. This is because the enmity between the snake's offspring and the woman's offspring foreshadows the conflict between Christ and Satan. The New Testament gives only the briefest support for this in reference to God crushing Satan under the feet of Christians (Rom 16:20). It is possible that God's Son being born of a woman also recalls this prediction (Gal 4:4). The word of curse on the snake implies grace to the human race and a recovery from the fall.[6]

As for when this promise was enacted, by reading Genesis 3:15 one may reach the conclusion that the promise was given as a reaction to the events that led to the banishment of Adam and Eve from the Garden of Eden instead of a pre-formed plan in God's mind beforehand. Another goal of this work is to investigate and dissect the implications of the promise given to Eve that through her seed retribution to the snake and redemption to mankind would be found. Still another objective this work seeks to

---

5   J.E. Smith, *The Pentateuch* (Joplin, MO: College Press Pub. Co., 1993), Genesis 3:15.

6   Graeme Goldsworthy, *According to Plan: The Unfolding Revelation of God in the Bible* (Downers Grove, IL: InterVarsity Press, 1991), 106.

achieve is a thorough investigation of the implications that this promise has concerning the dispensations and especially how this promise relates to the Covenant of Grace. In the letter of Paul to Titus, Paul gives a hint as to the length of time this promise had already been in place prior to the announcement in Genesis 3. He states in Titus, "in the hope of eternal life that God, who cannot lie, promised before time began, and has in His own time revealed His message in the proclamation that I was entrusted with by the command of God our Savior (Titus 1:2-3):[7]" The promise of eternal life was clearly made before time began. What does this mean in light of Covenant Theology? Is this a New Covenant called the Covenant of Redemption? What does this mean in light of Dispensationalism? Does the demarcation of a Dispensation of Innocence to a Dispensation of Conscience have significant implications? This work will investigate the answers to these questions as well as investigate a few of the major points of disagreements among a few of the tenets of each system before offering a distinctive alternative that best explains the biblical material concerning the subjects covered. An exhaustive sweep of every point of doctrine is too lofty a goal, but with a few tenets of each examined, hopefully a well rounded picture of what a Covenantal Dispensationalist (if there is to be such a person) might believe concerning the tenets addressed will emerge.

In addition, this work will show how the promise originally mentioned by God in Genesis 3 progresses through the Bible. Various covenants and promises made to Abraham, Moses, David, and the houses of Israel and Judah will be investigated to see if a unifying theme is present that would do justice to both Covenant Theology

---

7   *The Holy Bible : Holman Christian Standard Version.* (Nashville: Holman Bible Publishers, 2003), Tit 1:2-3. Unless otherwise noted, all Scripture references used are from the Holman Christian Standard Version.

PART I.
COVENANT THEOLOGY

CHAPTER 1

INTRODUCTION TO COVENANT THEOLOGY

Before one can understand how Covenant Theology differentiates itself from Dispensationalism, an investigation of Covenant Theology must take place including what the basic tenets are and, more importantly, how these tenets are wedded to the biblical repository. How each school deals with the covenants of the Bible and the economies of the Bible, whether explicitly stated or not, must be understood when one wishes to synchronize the two approaches into a more biblical model of interpretation. Also, a history of theological thought and development for each school should be examined. The first section of this work will focus on Covenant Theology.

The term "covenant" is a biblical term. The general definition of covenant as it appears in the Bible is as follows:

> A contract or agreement between two parties. In the Old Testament the Hebrew word *berith* is always

thus translated. *Berith* is derived from a root which means "to cut," and hence a covenant is a "cutting," with reference to the cutting or dividing of animals into two parts, and the contracting parties passing between them, in making a covenant (Gen. 15; Jer. 34:18, 19).

The corresponding word in the New Testament Greek is *diatheke*, which is, however, rendered "testament" generally in the Authorized Version. It ought to be rendered, just as the word *berith* of the Old Testament, "covenant."[8]

Covenant is used in various ways throughout Scripture, but the premise of the hermeneutical school of Covenant Theology is not entirely based on these biblical covenants. While the approach may or not be biblical, the covenants of Covenant Theology do not correspond in a one-to-one manner with the covenants in Scripture, but instead to over-arching covenants or meta-covenants. The covenants in Covenant Theology are more adequately called "Theological Covenants" as opposed to "Biblical Covenants."

Within the world of Covenant Theology, a good starting point would be a study of what a covenant meant in biblical times. Robert Bradshaw summarizes the history of covenant making in the ancient Near East:

Archaeology has provided us with examples of covenants from all over the Ancient Near East, dating from around 750 BC as far back as the third Millennium. Two main types of covenant are evident. The first is an agreement between equals called a *parity* agreement. . . The second, between

---

8   M. Easton, *Easton's Bible Dictionary* (Oak Harbor, WA: Logos Research Systems, Inc., 1996, c1897).

a Lord and his vassal, is known as a *suzerainty* or *vassal* treaty. Typically the parties of the former type of covenant refer to each other as "brothers", while parties to the second call themselves "Lord" and "Son".[9]

An example of the parity treaty is found between Solomon and Hiram of Tyre:

> This is probably the best scriptural example of a parity treaty. Hiram King of Tyre established friendly relations with David and his son Solomon (2 Sam. 5:11; 1 Kings 5:1-2). In return for timber and gold (9:11, 14) for the temple Solomon provided food for Hiram's household (5:3-11). They cemented their friendship by making a covenant (5:12). Later in 1 Kings we learn that Solomon had become deeply indebted to Hiram and gave him 20 towns on the Phoenician-Galilee border in payment. Hiram seems to have been unimpressed by the deal and addresses Solomon in the typical language of a parity treaty as "my brother" (9:10-14).[10]

Here we see the "brotherly" language of a parity treaty among equals. Each partner in the covenant has obligations to fulfill to the other. Another such example is a treaty between Ahab and Ben-Hadad:

> While seeking terms of surrender for their master Ben-Hadad's officials were surprised to hear Ahab speak of their master using the language usually reserved for partners in a parity treaty. Taking up the same theme they ensure Ben-Hadad's safety

---

9   Robert I. Bradshaw, "Covenant," http://www.biblicalstudies.org.uk/article_covenant.html, 1998 (accessed 12/10/2009).

10   Ibid.

and a treaty is made between him and Ahab (1 Kings 20:31-34). Ahab spared his life, an action that brought prophetic condemnation (20:35-42) and in the long term was ill-advised. In the short term it had advantages as it led to a military alliance and the return of captured Israelite cities which his father, Tabrimmon, had captured, as well as the establishment of Israelite bazaars and extra-territorial rights in Damascus. The peace thus established lasted for three years. During these years the states of Israel, Aram, Hamath and nine other smaller powers were forced to unite against the growing power of Assyria, which had been rendered impotent for almost two centuries by the attacks of Aramean nomads. From 900 BC onwards the power of Assyria swept westwards and in 853 Shalmaneser III faced the coalition of Syrian and Cilician states at Qarqar on the Orontes river. According to Shalmaneser's own records Ben-Hadad fielded 20,000 soldiers, and Ahab 10,000 soldiers and 2,000 chariots. "Shalmaneser claims a sweeping victory; the corpses of his foes, he says, covered the plain of the Orontes and dammed the stream itself. But the fact that he did not pursue his alleged advantage and returned home and did not return for 12 years suggests that the confederates gave a good account of themselves."[11] After the Assyrian threat had been vanquished, for a time at least, the alliance soon broke up and war resumed between Israel and Aram (22:1-4).[12]

---

11 F.F. Bruce, *Israel and the Nations* (Carlisle: Paternoster Press, c1963, 1987), 47. Quoted by Bradshaw in his article, "Covenant."

12 Bradshaw.

The second type of treaty, the *suzerainty* or *vassal* treaty is more appropriate in understanding the various covenants within Covenant Theology. This type of covenant is present in two of the three covenants that comprise Covenant Theology. An example of a suzerainty treaty in Scripture is found in Joshua. It is here where "the Gibeonites deceived Joshua into making a covenant with them. However, once made it could not be broken (Josh. 9:3-27). In the time of David, the Lord brought a famine on the land as a result of Saul breaking this covenant (2 Sam. 21:1-3)."[13] The two covenants of Covenant Theology which follow this model are the Covenant of Works and the Covenant of Grace. The Covenant of Redemption, because it involves at least two members of the trinity aligns better with a *parity* treaty. The members of the Godhead are co-equal and therefore the treaty, or covenant, made among them is not likened to a *vassal* treaty.[14]

One aspect of Covenant Theology that deserves comment even before investigating the general tenets of the system is the lack of the dividing line common to evangelicals when splitting covenants. The two major covenants, or testaments, that Christians agree upon and almost all Bibles split into two are notably absent when discussing the covenants of Covenant Theology. While the Covenant of Redemption will be shown to cover a time period encompassing the entirety of the Old and New Testaments, the Covenant of Works resides completely in the Old Testament, not even spanning the entire length of one biblical book, while the covenant grace covers most of the Old and the entire New

---

13   Ibid.

14   For a detailed treatment of the basic elements of these type of Late Bronze Age Hittite treaties, see George Mendenhall, George & Gary A. Heiron 1992. "Covenant," David Noel Freedman, Editor-in-Chief, *Anchor Bible Dictionary*, Vol. 1. London: Doubleday.

Testament. But the two most recognized covenantal divisions are absent from the scheme. The reason which will become clear is that the New Testament is not the sole domain for the Covenant of Grace. This covenant was not inaugurated at Christ's first coming, but will be shown to be foretold in very primitive form in the Garden of Eden and then more fully developed in Jeremiah. Dispensationalism comes closer to recognizing the break between the Testaments as a signal of a change in God's program, broadly, but not exactly separating the Dispensation of the Law with the dispensation of the Church (or grace) at the change in the Testaments. For the New Testament does not contain the entire Dispensation of Grace and the Millennium is considered a different dispensation entirely, and therefore the New Testament is not, in its entirety, a complete unit in either system.

Before examining the constituent parts of the covenants that comprise the three major covenants of Covenant Theology, this work now examines the history of Covenant Theology.

CHAPTER 2

HISTORY OF COVENANT THEOLOGY

As with any theological doctrine, the consistency of the respective adherents to a given doctrine to find commonalities and agreed upon principles, tenets, and views varies widely among those who claim to be a part of a particular camp. Covenant Theology is no exception to this rule. For the sake of space, the focus of this work will be upon the more generalized understanding of Covenant Theology, with the differences in particular planks on the platform tabled of necessity for the present discussion. J. Ligon Duncan provides a brief, but thorough understanding of what Covenant Theology is:

> Covenant Theology is the Gospel set in the context of God's eternal plan of communion with his people, and its historical outworking in the covenants of works and grace (as well as in the various progressive stages of the Covenant of Grace). Covenant Theology explains the meaning of the death of Christ in light of the fullness of the biblical teaching on the divine

covenants, undergirds our understanding of the nature and use of the sacraments, and provides the fullest possible explanation of the grounds of our assurance.

To put it another way, Covenant Theology is the Bible's way of explaining and deepening our understanding of: (1) the atonement [the meaning of the death of Christ]; (2) assurance [the basis of our confidence of communion with God and enjoyment of his promises]; (3) the sacraments [signs and seals of God's covenant promises — what they are and how they work]; and (4) the continuity of redemptive history [the unified plan of God's salvation]. Covenant Theology is also an hermeneutic, an approach to understanding the Scripture — an approach that attempts to biblically explain the unity of biblical revelation.[15]

A historical understanding of how the system developed will be helpful in gaining insight into the particulars that define one as a covenantalist. Covenant Theology, as systematized, is of fairly recent origin when considering the history of the Church.

Before heading into the history of Covenant Theology, some definitions will be helpful. J. Oliver Buswell, representative of Calvinistic Covenantalists, defines his understanding of Covenant Theology while including the dictionary definition:

The Latin noun *foedus*, from which the word 'federal' comes, means covenant, treaty, compact etc...

---

15 J. Ligon Duncan, "What is Covenant Theology" http://www.fpcjackson.org/resources/apologetics/Covenant%20Theology%20&%20Justification/ligoncovt.htm (accessed 12/22/2009).

The word 'covenant' (Hebrew *berith*, Greek *diatheke*) is used frequently throughout the Bible. Any arrangement more or less formerly instituted between two or more parties may be called a covenant. Sometimes a covenant is a mere promise and does not involve either conditions or consent on the part of the party or parties to whom the promise is made; but more frequently a covenant involves an arrangement, either tacit or explicit, between two or more parties, and involves conditional terms.

The theological system which rests upon the conception that before the fall, man was under the Covenant of Works, wherein God promised him (through Adam, the federal head of the race) eternal blessedness if he perfectly kept the law; and that since the fall man is under a Covenant of Grace, wherein God, of His free grace, promises the same blessings to all who believe in Christ (the federal head of the Church)."[16]

Paul Enns describes Covenant Theology in this way:
Covenant Theology is a system of interpreting the Scriptures on the basis of two covenants: the Covenant of Works and the Covenant of Grace. Some Covenant theologians specify three covenants: works, redemption, and grace. Covenant Theology teaches that God initially made a Covenant of Works with Adam, promising eternal life for obedience and death for disobedience. Adam failed, and death entered the human race. God, however, moved to resolve man's dilemma by entering into a Covenant

---

16   J. Oliver Buswell, *Systematic Theology of the Christian Religion* (Grand Rapids: Zondervan, 1962), 307.

of Grace through which the problem of sin and death would be overcome. Christ is the ultimate mediator of God's Covenant of Grace.[17]

Diversity among adherents is common to both systems, and perhaps the greatest divergence in Covenant Theology is between the Covenant of Grace and the Covenant of Redemption. At times the two are used interchangeably, but for the purpose of this work, the context regarding the Covenant of Grace will follow what Buswell and Enns have said above; that the Covenant of Grace is chronologically subsequent to the Covenant of Works. Some dispute exists as to the validity of the Covenant of Redemption. The evidence for a Covenant of Redemption is not explicit in Scripture and must be derived. Chafer writes about this concerning the lack of evidence, "This covenant rests upon slight revelation. It is rather sustained largely by the fact that it seems both reasonable and inevitable."[18] But as will be shown, the Covenant of Works and the Covenant of Grace are on as soft a footing as the Covenant of Redemption - as the biblical record and even Covenantalists will attest to.

The author of the Second Helvetic Confession, Johann Heinrich Bullinger (1504–1575) played a large role in the development of Covenant Theology. He taught about federal theology which is a significant tenet of Covenant Theology and will be expounded upon below. Second only to John Calvin, he was a leader within the Reformed Church.[19]

17   Paul P. Enns, *The Moody Handbook of Theology* (Chicago: IL: Moody Press, 1997, c1989), 503.

18   Lewis S. Chafer, *Systematic Theology* (Dallas, TX: Dallas Seminary Press, 1947), 1:42.

19   Philip Schaff, *The Creeds of Christendom with a History and Critical Notes, 3 Volumes* (Grand Rapids: Baker, 1977), 3:831-909.

The two major covenants, that of works and that of grace, can be traced in origin to Johannes Wollebius (1586-1629) in his work *Compendium of Christian Theology*. Thoroughly reformed, Wollebius picked up Bullinger's federal theology and first articulated the now-essential teaching of two major covenants, both of which were/are initiated by God and with stipulations placed upon man.[20] Geoffrey W. Bromiley says about Wollebius:

> Wollebius taught that God made a Covenant of Works with Adam in which God ruled over man before the Fall. Wollebius defined the Covenant of Works as it has usually been defined: "the promise of eternal life for obedience and the threat of death for disobedience." Wollebius understood the two trees in the garden as sacraments of the Covenant of Works.
>
> Wollebius also taught a Covenant of Grace, made through God's mercy after the Fall. The Covenant of Grace, which extends across all ages after the Fall, is mediated by Christ. Wollebius referred to two administrations, the Old Testament and the New Testament. The Old Testament covered three ages: Adam to Abraham, Abraham to Moses, and Moses to Christ. The new administration is the period after Christ's coming. Wollebius emphasized five distinctions between the two administrations of the Old and New Testaments. The sacraments of the Covenant of Works are circumcision and the Passover ceremony in the Old Testament

---

20   Geoffrey W. Bromily, *Historical Theology: An Introduction* (Grand Rapids: Eerdmans, 1978), 306-14.

and baptism and the Lord's Supper in the New Testament.[21]

While clearly the sacramental aspects of Wollebius' theology did not gain traction, his chronology concerning the time periods under which the two covenants were in force was landmark on future Covenantalists.

Another early influence on Covenant Theology was William Ames (1576-1633). Ames was a Puritan who stood strongly against Arminianism. His influence on the Synod of Dort which was a major milestone for Calvinism begins to show the influence Calvinism had and continues to have on Covenant Theology. This is unfortunate as the marrying of Covenant Theology to Calvinism has left a good number of Dispensationalists that hold to the five points of Calvinism with a more challenging effort to ingratiate to either the Calvinist camp or the Arminian camp. However, the issues between the two opposing theological traditions of Calvinism and Arminianism are not of primary concern to the present exploration into either Covenant Theology or Dispensationalism and ample evidence abounds that Dispensationalists of all stripes have been adherents of Calvinism, Arminianism, and all points in between.[22] Bromiley writes of Ames:

> Ames, like Wollebius, taught a Covenant of Works established before the Fall. Ames, however, held

---

21 Ibid.

22 Two examples of Calvinistic Dispensationalists would be John MacArthur, who explains his understanding of Dispensationalism at http://www.middletownBibleChurch.org/dispen/jmacdis.htm (accessed 10/28/2009), and Arthur Pink, whose eschatology appears dispensational, despite his opposition to Dispensationalism as commonly understood. See his book, *A Study in Dispensationalism,* available for free with several of his writings at http://www.pbministries.org/books/pink/Dispensationalism/Dispensationalism.htm.

that the Covenant of Works, which was universal in scope, continued after the Fall. Its fulfillment was dependent upon man's obedience to God. Some theologians would place the continuation of the covenant idea under the covenant of law rather than suggesting it belongs to the Covenant of Works.

Ames taught a Covenant of Grace made after the Fall, but he preferred to call it a testament because it was related to the death of Christ. Ames saw God as the lone participant in the Covenant of Grace. He taught a universal sufficiency in the covenant but an application that is limited to those for whom God intended it. Ames also understood the Covenant of Grace to extend across all ages after the Fall. Ames taught that the Covenant of Grace spanned two administrations, the Old Testament and the New Testament; the Old Testament covered two ages— before Moses and after Moses; the New Testament also covers two ages—from Christ to the end of the world, and the end itself. The end will achieve the purpose of the covenant: God's glory and man's salvation. The sign of the Covenant of Grace is baptism, hence, infants should be baptized.[23]

Here we see one of the knots that need to be untangled when thinking about covenants and dispensations. Ames is one of the first, but certainly not the last, theologians to discuss various dispensations in light of covenants, even if here he prefers testaments and uses the term administrations; a synonym for dispensations. While the groundwork for Dort that Ames help to lay cannot be dismissed nor discarded,

---

23   Bromiley, *Historical Theology*, 314.

his views on infant baptism and the Covenant of Works extending beyond Adam are not picked up by all Reformers and certainly not by Dispensationalists. The extension of the Covenant of Works past the dispensation of innocence in the Garden of Eden is an outlier on the Covenant Theology map and will not be examined. Infant baptism is dealt with in an excursus at the end of this chapter.

Covenant Theology was moving out of infancy and into a clearly defined hermeneutic by the time of Johannes Cocceius (1603–1669). Cocceius had a great deal of influence on the burgeoning Covenant Theology movement that began during the Reformation. Heppe describes Cocceius' theology in *Reformed Dogmatics:*

> Cocceius taught that God entered into a Covenant of Works with Adam.[24] This covenant enabled Adam to enjoy communion and friendship with God. Cocceius taught that Adam represented the entire human race in the Covenant of Works. If Adam obeyed God, he would come to a knowledge and sense of his own good; if he disobeyed, he would rush headlong into evil, or death. The tree of life was the "sacrament of the heavenly city and of eternal life" according to Cocceius. Because Christ is life, the tree of life signified the Son of God. Through his sin, Adam became guilty, fell from God's fellowship, from hope of eternal life, from spiritual grace, from uprightness, from authority over creatures, and from physical life.

---

24   See the extend discussion of Cocceius's teaching on the Covenant of Works in Heinrich Heppe, *Reformed Dogmatics* (Grand Rapids: Baker, 1978), 281-319.

Cocceius taught a universalistic basis for the Covenant of Grace.[25] God resolved to show His inexpressible mercy and "to employ an ineffable kindness and longsuffering towards the entire human race." But this had to be through a mediator who alone could atone for sin. Christ's death was "a guarantee which was already effective from the start, even before the Son, in view of this merit of his in the future, had fulfilled his vow by completing the work of redemption. Although the Son had not yet plucked out the guilt of sin, it was no longer reckoned unto them." This became a point of controversy for Cocceius. Cocceius also distinguished a "twofold time," the first was in the Old Testament "in expectation of Christ," whereas in the New Testament it was "in faith in Christ revealed." But Cocceius emphasized that in both Old Testament and New Testament eras, people were always saved by grace.[26]

Cocceius has clarified even further what is at the heart of Covenant Theology – God saves sinners by His gracious choice. The schema under which He does this is aptly termed by Cocceius as the "Covenant of Grace." The concept of the Covenant of Redemption is present with Cocceius, if not the terminology and looking backwards on it we see the commingling of the two covenants present. Also, there is no hint with the early proponents of Covenant Theology what has become characteristic and synonymous with the movement, that of allegorizing Scripture instead of reading Scripture in a literal, commonsense fashion.

---

25 Ibid., 371.
26 Heppe is quoted in P.P. Enns, 504.

Kerry Trahan recounts the way in which each system has been cast in the current debate into an either/or choice between the literal or allegorical method of interpretation:

> Although *spiritually* kindred in relationship, many *doctrinal* issues (such as views concerning Israel and the Church, the Millennium, the Rapture, etc.) set these two opposing *theological* camps apart. The distinctions result primarily from the manner in which each interprets the Bible: the covenant theologian interprets the Scriptures *allegorically*, while Dispensationalists on the other hand, employ the *consistent literal* method of interpretation.[27]

Below it will be shown that the more biblical approach when reading the Bible is with an eye towards the most plain, literal reading. In reading the Bible plainly, however; one does not need to exclude the covenants of God, including the theological covenants when considering God's management of mankind throughout the different dispensations that occur in the Bible. This type of Covenant Theology as understood in the infancy of Covenant Theology is in no way contradictory to the Dispensationalist's idea of God relating to man in different ways at different times.

As this brief survey relating the historical roots of Covenant Theology has shown, the major tenets of Covenant Theology have found expression fairly recently when considering the history of the Church and appear innocuous as described above. As the doctrines swirled about, perhaps no greater document outlines what is still today to be considered the bedrock of Covenant Theology, the Westminster Confession of 1647. And within the

---

27 Kerry Trahan, *A Complete Guide to Understanding the Dispensationalism Controversy* (Port Neches, TX: Disciple of Jesus Ministries, Inc., 2007), 31.

Confession terms such as dispensations and covenants are found in close proximity without the slightest hint of contradiction. Part of Confession reads as follows:

    1. The distance between God and His creation is so great, that, although reasoning creatures owe Him obedience as their creator, they nonetheless could never realize any blessedness or reward from Him without His willingly condescending to them. And so it pleased God to provide for man by means of covenants.

    2. The first covenant made with man was a Covenant of Works. In it life was promised to Adam and through him to his descendants, on the condition of perfect, personal obedience.

    3. By his fall, man made himself incapable of life under that covenant, and so the Lord made a second, the Covenant of Grace. In it He freely offers sinners life and salvation through Jesus Christ. In order to be saved He requires faith in Jesus and promises to give His Holy Spirit to everyone who is ordained to life so that they may be willing and able to believe.

    4. This Covenant of Grace is frequently identified in Scripture as a testament, in reference to the death of Jesus Christ, the testator, and to the everlasting inheritance and everything included in that legacy.

    5. This covenant was administered differently in the time of the law and in the time of the gospel. Under the law it was administered by promises, prophecies,

sacrifices, circumcision, the paschal lamb, and other types and ordinances given to the Jewish people, all foreshadowing Christ. For that time the covenant administered under the law through the operation of the Spirit was sufficient and effective in instructing the elect and building up their faith in the promised Messiah, by Whom they had full remission of their sins and eternal salvation. This administration is called the Old Testament.

6. Under the gospel Christ Himself, the substance of God's grace, was revealed. The ordinances of this New Testament are the preaching of the word and the administration of the sacraments of baptism and the Lord's supper. Although these are fewer in number and are administered with more simplicity and less outward glory, yet they are available to all nations, Jews and Gentiles, and in them the spiritual power of the Covenant of Grace is more fully developed. There are not then two essentially different covenants of grace, but one and the same covenant under different dispensations.[28]

What this statement demonstrates is that there was a time when dispensations and covenants could live side by side. The statement, "One and the same covenant under different dispensations" shows that Covenant Theology in its initial forms understood and embraced the distinction between dispensations. Admittedly, this was set against no rival theological school such as exists now by the name of Dispensationalism. The modern day tenets of

---

28   Douglas Kelly et al., eds., *The Westminster Confession of Faith: A New Edition* (Greenwood, SC: Attic, 1981), 13-4.

Dispensationalism were far from formalized at this point, but little would be in dispute concerning the major tenets. Obviously such issues as the application of grace in the sacraments would be taken up, as well as more probing about Israel/Church distinctions, but the basic idea of different dispensations is present even if modern day Covenantalists would reject that the *Confession* teaches or is any way in harmony with Dispensationalism. Properly understood, however, dispensational distinctions are found in the early teachings of Covenant Theology and the harmony between these two schools of interpretation needs to be reestablished.

While federal headship, that of Adam in the first covenant, and Christ in the second is clearly demonstrated in the above *Confession*, nowhere is mention made of an eternal covenant made between the Father and the Son. Only the covenants of law and grace are mentioned. This could relate to the later development of the Covenant of Redemption in the history of Covenant Theology as the evidence is even more conjectural in the case of redemption than it is in the covenants of works and grace.

The views of modern day Covenantalists are generally compatible with these views. Note that a biblical hermeneutic was not in the Reformers' explanations of what Covenant Theology was meant to accomplish. For the most part, Covenant Theology was not an effort to allegorize or spiritualize the Bible, but a way of understanding the overall story of the Bible and to help the reader understand how God redeems humanity; how the expression of this love was accomplished during different administrations or dispensations. The Covenant of Redemption, as described below, fits perfectly well with the overall goal of Covenant Theology and with Dispensationalism. The goal, then, of Covenant Theology appears to be a way of explaining God's activity in salvation during different periods of time and that God has always had but one way to save mankind, by grace through faith.

EXCURSUS: INFANT BAPTISM

Earlier in this chapter William Ames was shown to be a proponent of infant baptism and argued that infant baptism is a sign of the Covenant of Grace, therefore it follows, according to Ames, that it is not only appropriate, but biblically correct to baptize infants. Most Covenantalists have carried forward this view, especially through Reformed theology. The issue of whether or not to baptize infants versus the baptism of confessed believers is one where agreement is rarely seen across the aisle between Covenant Theology and Dispensationalism and is often the dividing issue among denominations. The history of the Baptists is stained with blood that was shed over opposition to this practice.[29] Unfortunately, the limits of space prevent a detailed refutation of infant baptism, but to say that infant baptism is closely linked with Reformed theology is not a new revelation. Paul K. Jewett has written on the subject from a Covenant Theology perspective, and does a nice job of relating the history of infant baptism through the history of the Western Church and the Eastern Church.[30] Unfortunately, the scriptural support for such a position is non-existent. It will suffice here to say that baptism is virtually absent prior to John the Baptist, and no covenantalist would deny that the Covenant of Grace extends backwards from the cross and reaches back to at least Moses, if not Abraham

---

29   For a detailed history of the persecutions of Anabaptists, see William Estep's *The Anabaptist Story* (Grand Rapids: Eerdmans, 1996).

30   Paul K. Jewett, *Infant Baptism and the Covenant of Grace* (Grand Rapids: Eerdmans, 1980).

or further. Covenantalists, like J. Ligon Duncan, see infant baptism as a sacrament, or a sign or seal of God's covenant promises administered to those of the faith community. While logically this may make sense, it is unbiblical and not related to the ordinance of believer's baptism which is patterned in the New Testament.

The argument from Colossians 2:11-12, with its close proximity and seemingly juxtaposition of circumcision and baptism, is not as forceful as those who see continuity between the Old and New Covenants would like it to be.

Colossians 2:11-12 reads, "In Him you were also circumcised with a circumcision not done with hands, by putting off the body of flesh, in the circumcision of the Messiah. Having been buried with Him in baptism, you were also raised with Him through faith in the working of God, who raised Him from the dead." The term "circumcision of Christ" refers to a spiritual circumcision. This circumcision is effected through Christ. [31] While the argument would be that baptism is the next action depicted after the mention of spiritual baptism, therefore linking them together, this is fatally flawed. The baptism refers to the actual act of baptizing a believer, and this cannot happen before a person becomes part of the community of faith (i.e. places faith in Jesus Christ). To say that baptizing an infant is linked to circumcision is to miss Paul's point altogether. The circumcision that is evidenced by the sign of baptism takes place at the moment of faith, with baptism being an outward expression of this occurrence. Because the covenant Christ makes is only with believers, it is completely different from a Jewish male infant being baptized to show they are part of the covenant family of Abraham. Not all those that are descendents of Abraham are part of the eternal promise of

---

31   M.R. Vincent, *Word Studies in the New Testament* (Bellingham, WA: Logos Research Systems, Inc., 2002), 3:488.

CHAPTER 3

TENETS OF COVENANT THEOLOGY

At the very heart of Covenant Theology are God's grace and its expression to a group of people who do not adequately reciprocate the type of faithfulness God has shown to them. This extension of grace is made to everyone who believes upon the Lord Jesus Christ. This fundamental principle answers the basic need of everyone who is under the condemnation of Adam. The relationship between God and His Creation on an individual level or a corporate level must answer the same question the Philippian jailer asked in Acts 16:30, and is of vital importance to every man, woman and child who lives upon this earth, "What must I do to be saved?"

Throughout the history of Covenant Theology, all definitions that attempt to explain the theological system are in essence attempts to understand the application of salvation to all of God's elect who are under the curse of death due to Adam and the Fall. God's redemption as explained in a series of two covenants tries to describe as adequately as possible the biblical narrative of God's forgiveness and redemption; the deliverance offered through Christ from the punishment of spiritual death. The salvific plan of God in Covenant Theology cannot be overemphasized; as the covenantal underpinning is the essence of why there is a need for the covenants of grace and by extension the Covenant of Redemption. However, before the praise for Covenant Theology's exceptional soteriological benefits can be assumed, there are some troubling problems inherent in the covenant understanding of salvation during the era before Christ. As will be demonstrated, neither school of interpretation has a more biblical approach to pre-Christ election and salvation than the other school. Ryrie calls attention to this problem when defending Dispensationalism against the same charge:

> We have pointed out that Dispensationalists are charged with teaching two or more ways of salvation. One would think that this charge could never be leveled against Covenant Theology since its Covenant of Grace supposedly governs the way of salvation from Genesis 3:15 to the end of the Bible. Indeed, this pouring of the grace of God into a strait-jacket is, according to the Dispensationalists, the weakness of the covenant position.

> But what does the covenant theologian do with the matter of salvation under the law? Berkhof declares that "grace offers escape from the low only as a condition of salvation – as it is in the Covenant of Works – from the curse of the law." In another

place he says, "From the law . . . both as a means of obtaining eternal life and as a condemning power believers are set free in Christ."[32] Allis declares positively, "The law is a declaration of the will of God for man's salvation."[33] Even Payne, a covenant Premillennialist, for all his effort to keep from indicating that salvation during the period of the law was by any means other than God's forgiveness in anticipation of the work of Christ, apparently slips at one point: "From the Mosaic period and onward, nonpresumptuous sins (Lev. 5:3) were specifically forgiven via the ritual law (v. 10;cf. Ps. 19:13); and other intentional violations were included as well (cf. Lev. 5:1, 4)."[34]

These are very odd statements to find in the writings of Covenant theologians if, as they say, "salvation has always been one and the same: having the same promise, the same Saviour, the same condition, the same salvation."[35] Indeed, the law was a declaration of the will of God for man's salvation, and if sins could be forgiven via the ritual law, then Covenant Theology must be teaching two ways of salvation — one by law and one by grace![36]

---

32   Louis Berkhof, *Systematic Theology* (Grand Rapids: Eerdmans, 1941), 291, 614. Quoted in Ryrie, *Dispensationalism*.

33   Oswald T. Allis, *Prophecy and the Church* (Philadelphia: Presbyterian and Reformed, 1945), 39. Quoted in Ryrie, *Dispensationalism*.

34   J. Barton Payne, *The Theology of the Older Testament* (Grand Rapids: Zondervan, 1962), 414. Quoted in Ryrie, *Dispensationalism*.

35   Charles Hodge, *Systematic Theology* (Grand Rapids: Eerdmans, 1946), 2:368. Quoted in Ryrie, *Dispensationalism*.

36   Charles Ryrie, *Dispensationalism* (Chicago: Moody Publishers, 2007), 224-5.

Obviously this indictment is somewhat overblown, but serves to prove the point. The vast majority of Covenantalists have revised such positions, in the same way early Dispensationalists have revised certain aspects of the Israel/Church distinctions. So what is the main thrust of Covenant Theology if salvation is as unclear as a major premise in Covenant Theology as it is accused of in Dispensationalism? The answer is the continuity between the testaments. The continuity is present between the Old and New Testaments. The promise of a New Covenant which completes the Covenant of Grace is to be found in the Old Testament, while the fulfillment of the promise is in the New Testament, but there is continuity as "one" people of God; primarily expressed through Israel in the Old Testament and then through the Church in the New Testament. Although Christ radically changed the way in which people now related to God and to each other, this change is not so radical, in a Covenantal theologian's understanding, as to break the continuity of the overall Covenant of Grace begun in Genesis 3. It is in this passage in Genesis that the promise that will ultimately be fulfilled in Christ first finds allusion. In a sense, all that transpires after the initial promise is in continuous contact to the first representation of the promise. Standing in opposition to the perceived radical discontinuity of Dispensationalism, the themes of continuity and discontinuity are expressed by Feinberg as thus:

> "Theological positions can be placed on a continuum running from views holding to absolute continuity between the Testaments to views holding to absolute discontinuity between the Testaments. The more one moves in the continuity direction, the more covenantal he becomes; and the more he moves in

the discontinuity direction, the more dispensational he becomes."[37]

W.A. Elwell and B.J. Beitzel demonstrate how far modern theology has come in separating the two hermeneutical schools:

> Difficult issues complicate the question of the relationship between the two Testaments. What is the exact connection between Law and grace, or between Israel and the Church? Two poles have developed: Dispensationalism, which teaches a dichotomy between the two, with the Church Age an additional historical phase not anticipated by the Old Testament and Reformed or Covenant Theology, which maintains an implicit continuity between the two, with the Church Age ushered in by the work of Christ and continuing the divine plan. Dispensationalism holds that the OT Law has been replaced by New Testament grace; Covenant Theology states that the Law has been fulfilled in grace.[38]

Here we see a few erroneous facts that need to be addressed in order to systemize a proper understanding of both Covenant Theology and Dispensationalism, as Elwell and Beitzel oversimplify and corrupt slightly the teachings of each school. When contemplating Covenant Theology in such a manner as described above, a crucial error is made. Elwell and Beitzel state that Covenant Theology is

---

37   John S. Feinberg, editor, *Continuity and Discontinuity: Perspectives on the Relationship Between the Old and New Testaments* (Wheaton, IL: Crossway, 1988), xii.

38   W. A. Elwell and B. J. Beitzel, *Baker Encyclopedia of the Bible* (Grand Rapids, MI: Baker Book House, 1988), 346.

reserved for the Reformed theologian only, as if Reformed persons could not hold to such a view as Dispensationalism. Interestingly, Dispensationalists often wrongly accuse Covenant Theology of holding to "Replacement Theology", whereas the definition, as understood by Elwell and Beitzel states that the Church does not so much "replace" Israel, instead the definition of Covenant Theology says merely that the "Law has been fulfilled in grace." While this is certainly true, we begin to see the ways in which the two camps misrepresent the other camp's views. The problems with Dispensationalism found above will be tabled until a later chapter. So what of this helps lay down workable tenets of Covenant Theology? Sadly, not much. The implicit continuity between Israel and the Church is here stated, and that is certainly of deep importance to Covenant Theology and is true of Dispensationalism as well. To this, the author, along with most orthodox Dispensationalists would agree. There is certainly some continuity between Israel and the Church. This does not make one of necessity a replacement of the other. The people of Israel who were elect and chosen by God are certainly to inherit the same blessings those in the Church will, but the nation Israel is merely a group of ethnically similar people descended from Abraham, some of whom are saved and some of whom are not in the eyes of the covenantalist. A disregard by the covenant theologian to Israel's place in God's redemptive plan is an oversight that needs correcting.

Therefore, the first tenet to be identified as distinctively covenantal is some type of continuity between the Old Testament and the New Testament. This is in alignment with Dispensationalism as we shall see, because the continuity deals with the basis on which mankind is eternally saved, by grace through faith, which is in complete harmony with Dispensationalism. This is not a New Testament idea, but it must be understood as present in the Old Testament only by looking backwards into time from the cross, where the salvation of Israel is promised through a coming Messiah. This would serve as a presupposition of a biblical hermeneutic, but not a presupposition that disqualifies a dispensational approach to Scripture. For even Dispensationalists, while recognizing dissimilarities in how God deals with mankind, not only with Israel and the Church, but also with Adam, Noah, and many others, note the similarities that permeate all dispensations, especially as it relates to how a man might be saved. Resolution must still occur in understanding how it is that God works differently with the same groups of people in different dispensations, such as modern Jews who accept Christ can and should join the Church, and how Gentiles in Israel would become "Jewish" during the Dispensation of the Law.

A. Covenant of Works (Genesis 1:1-3:15)

A brief overview of the three covenants that comprise Covenant Theology would be helpful to round out the discussion on the major tenants of Covenant Theology. The Covenant of Works is well defined by Heidegger in Heppe's *Reformed Dogmatics:*

The Covenant of Works is God's pact with Adam in his integrity, as the head of the whole human race, by which God requiring of man the perfect obedience of the law of works promised him if obedient eternal life in heaven, but threatened him if he transgressed with eternal death: and on his part man promised perfect obedience."[39]

---

39   Heinrich Heppe, *Reformed Dogmatics* (Grand Rapids: Baker Book House, 1978), 283.

The man with whom God has covenanted with in this covenant is Adam. He has a certain responsibility applicable to the dispensation in which he finds himself. In the case of Adam within the Garden of Eden, the responsibility for Adam is perfect obedience under threat of death. Adam here is the federal head of the entire human race. As the representative of all, as Adam does, so does all those he represents.

Paul draws a parallel between Adam and Christ in Romans 5:12-21:

> Therefore, just as sin entered the world through one man, and death through sin, in this way death spread to all men, because all sinned. 13 In fact, sin was in the world before the law, but sin is not charged to one's account when there is no law. 14 Nevertheless, death reigned from Adam to Moses, even over those who did not sin in the likeness of Adam's transgression. He is a prototype of the Coming One.

> 15 But the gift is not like the trespass. For if by the one man's trespass the many died, how much more have the grace of God and the gift overflowed to the many by the grace of the one man, Jesus Christ. 16 And the gift is not like the one man's sin, because from one sin came the judgment, resulting in condemnation, but from many trespasses came the gift, resulting in justification. 17 Since by the one man's trespass, death reigned through that one man, how much more will those who receive the overflow of grace and the gift of righteousness reign in life through the one man, Jesus Christ.

> 18 So then, as through one trespass there is condemnation for everyone, so also through

one righteous act there is life-giving justification for everyone. 19 For just as through one man's disobedience the many were made sinners, so also through the one man's obedience the many will be made righteous. 20 The law came along to multiply the trespass. But where sin multiplied, grace multiplied even more, 21 so that, just as sin reigned in death, so also grace will reign through righteousness, resulting in eternal life through Jesus Christ our Lord.

As Paul points out, in Adam all men have now died spiritually, and will die physically, but in Christ all those who are His are made alive. Christ is sometimes known as the second Adam and is in a similar role to Adam when Christ is placed into the context of being the one upon whom responsibilities are laid in the Covenant of Grace, only this time there is success rather than failure.

Adam's sin is called a transgression of the covenant directly in Hosea 6:7, "But they like men (Adam) have violated the covenant; there they have betrayed Me." There is considerable doubt whether this reference means the covenant between Adam as an individual and God. Some would argue that this is yet another theological covenant based on inference and reading back later passages into Genesis 1-3.[40] Another explanation, although an extremely unlikely one, is that Hosea refers to an otherwise unknown covenant violated by the people of a town called Adam that is on the banks of the Jordan (Joshua 3:16).[41] A more

---

40   So William J. Dumbrell, *Covenant and Creation: A Theology of Old Testament Covenants* (Nashville: Thomas Nelson, 1984), 44-46.

41   See Ernest Nicholson, *God and His People: Covenant and Theology in the Old Testament* (Oxford: Clarendon Press, 1998), 116. This is highly speculative and has against it the complete lack of any textual support.

possible, but still speculative, idea is that Adam should be translated "dirt" and thus the text should be rendered, "But they, like "dirt" have violated the covenant, there they have betrayed Me." This rendering would place the violation wholly within the Mosaic covenant.[42]

Even if Hosea is not an explicit proof text for the Covenant of Works, God clearly relates to Adam in a certain way for a particular period of time with particular parameters around his behavior. And although there is no specific mention of a covenant in the early chapters of Genesis, the existence of a covenant is arguably implied according to the definitions of covenant as outlined earlier. A covenant involves an agreement between two parties, in this case, between God and Adam in Genesis 2:16–17, where God laid down the terms of the covenant.[43] The covenant principle is also suggested in Leviticus 18:5; Ezekiel 20:11, 13, 20; Luke 10:28; Romans 7:10; 10:5; and Galatians 3:12.[44]

Paul P. Enns describes the predominant features of the Covenant of Works:

> ***Features.*** (1) The promise. The promise of the Covenant of Works was that if Adam obeyed the command of God he would not die; this is suggested from the negative statement of Genesis 2:17, "in the day that you eat from it you shall surely die." In other words, if Adam did not eat of the fruit, he would live. This promise to Adam is consistent with other passages that emphasize the covenant, or law, that man was placed under by God. The promise for obedience was not the mere continuation of mortal life because that was already his possession. "The

---

42   Douglas Stuart, "Hosea-Jonah," *Word Biblical Commentary*, Vol. 31 (Waco, TX: Word, 1987).

43   Berkhof, 213.

44   Ibid., 214, 216.

life thus promised included the happy, holy, and immortal existence of the soul and body,"[45] namely eternal life. This was "life raised to its highest development of perennial bliss and glory." [46]

(2) Condition. The condition God placed on Adam was perfect obedience. This is the condition for acceptance mentioned elsewhere in the Bible (cf. Gal. 3:10; James 2:10). Adam was instructed not to eat the fruit of the tree of the knowledge of good and evil (Gen. 2:17); that was the condition. The test was whether man would obey God or follow his own judgment. [47]

(3) Penalty. Punishment for disobedience to the Covenant of Works is stated in the term "die" (Gen. 2:17). [48] The term should be understood as comprehensive, including all penal evil. Death stands as the opposite of all that Adam was promised in life; Adam stood to forfeit physical, spiritual, and eternal life. "The life promised...includes all that is involved in the happy, holy, and immortal existence of the soul and body; and therefore death must include not only all the miseries of this life and the dissolution of the body, but also all that is meant by spiritual and eternal death." [49]

---

45   Charles Hodge, *Systematic Theology*, 3 vols. (Reprint. London: Clarke, 1960), 2:118.

46   Berkhof, 216.

47   Ibid., 217.

48   Hodge, *Systematic Theology*, 2:120.

49   Ibid.

(4) Present status of the Covenant of Works. This can be answered in a twofold manner. In one sense the Covenant of Works is not abrogated. God still demands perfect obedience of men, just as He did of Adam (Lev. 18:5; Rom. 10:5; Gal. 3:12); furthermore, the curse of death is evidence that the covenant is not abrogated. However, the covenant can be viewed as abrogated in the sense that its obligations are met in Christ.[50] So many Covenant theologians are very emphatic that the Covenant of Works is no longer in force.[51] [52]

Enns brings up another point that has implications for all the covenants and dispensations covering both hermeneutical schools. Has the Covenant of Works been abrogated? Are the stipulations still in effect? The answer to this question is yes and no. Yes in the sense that even one sin can separate us from the covenantal relationship we have with God, but no in the sense that Christ has fulfilled the requirements of the covenant and one can place their faith and trust in His completed work on the cross as having satisfied the stipulations of the covenant on behalf of all that transgress the covenant.

A final interesting facet of this covenant is its exact correlation to the Age of Innocence in Dispensationalism. The accusation against Dispensationalism that it teaches different ways of salvation in different dispensations is hereby clearly identified with a covenant where reward is eternal life and disobedience is death; the exact teaching that Covenantalists use against Dispensationalists. The truth is that to the extent God had different plans of salvation, if

---

50   Berkhof, 218.
51   Buswell, 1:312-14.
52   Enns, 507.

at all, the duration was brief, and no one was justified or condemned based on this "other" method. The truth is the Covenant of Grace has always governed the election of the saints regardless of whether one is a Dispensationalist or a covenant theologian.

B. Covenant of Grace (Genesis 3:16-Revelation 22:21)

The Covenant of Grace is the successor to and chronologically subsequent covenant under which man is able to participate in after the failure of Adam during the Covenant of Grace. Though a fuller exposition of stipulation, failure, and judgment will accompany the dispensational overview, it is important to note the similar feature in the dispensation of innocence, also known as the Covenant of Works. The Covenant of Grace, as Paul P. Enns described earlier, could be considered a continuation of the Covenant of Works, and is typically thought of as a covenant between God and each and every man and woman.

The Covenant of Works was between God and Adam, and all of mankind subsequent to Adam is born into this covenant and therefore shares in the punishment inflicted upon Adam for breaking the terms of the covenant. However, the Covenant of Grace has a more positive outlook. The covenant made by God is for all those who will accept Christ and is said to be either a covenant made with "the sinner" or the "elect sinner in Christ. [53]

Louis Berkhof highlights several of the features that are distinct concerning the Covenant of Grace:

(1) It is a gracious covenant. God provides His Son as a guarantee for our salvation; through His grace God enables man to meet the demands of the covenant responsibilities by the gift of the Holy Spirit. (2) It is a Trinitarian covenant.

---

53   Berkhof, 273.

The origin of the covenant is in the elective love of the Father, the redemption by the Son, and the application of the Holy Spirit (Eph. 1:3–14). (3) It is eternal and an unbreakable covenant. This covenant is unchangeable; God will forever be faithful to the covenant He has promised and provided. (4) It is a particular covenant. It is not a universal covenant because it does not extend to everyone; only the elect are the objects of the covenant. (5) It is the same in all dispensations. The summary phrase, "I will be God to you," is a unifying phrase in both the Old Testament and the New Testament (Gen. 17:7; Exodus. 19:5; 20:1; Deut. 29:13; 2 Sam. 7:14; Jer. 31:33; Heb. 8:10). This is further seen in that people are saved by the same gospel in all ages (Gal. 1:8–9). [54]

The Covenant of Redemption is explained in the next section, but the similarities are striking and one can see the interchangeableness of the two that takes place even without noticing by Covenant theologians. Charles Hodge explains how a person may find themselves in covenant with God under the gracious covenant extended from Genesis 3:16 through the return of Christ:

> The condition of the Covenant of Grace, so far as adults are concerned, is faith in Christ. That is, in order to partake of the benefits of this covenant we must receive the Lord Jesus Christ as the Son of God in whom and for whose sake its blessings are vouchsafed to the children of men. Until we thus believe we are aliens and strangers from the covenant of promise, without God and without Christ. We must acquiesce in this covenant, renouncing all other methods of salvation, and consenting to be

---

54 Ibid., 278-82.

saved on the terms which it proposes, before we are made partakers of its benefits. The word "condition," however, is used in two senses. Sometimes it means the meritorious consideration on the ground of which certain benefits are bestowed. In this sense perfect obedience was the condition of the covenant originally made with Adam. Had he retained his integrity he would have merited the promised blessing. For to him that worketh the reward is not of grace but of debt. In the same sense the work of Christ is the condition of the Covenant of Redemption. It was the meritorious ground, laying a foundation in justice for the fulfillment of the promises made to Him by the Father. But in other cases, by condition we merely mean a *sine qua non*. A blessing may be promised on condition that it is asked for; or that there is a willingness to receive it. There is no merit in the asking or in the willingness, which is the ground of the gift. It remains a gratuitous favour; but it is, nevertheless, suspended upon the act of asking. It is in this last sense only that faith is the condition of the Covenant of Grace. There is no merit in believing. It is only the act of receiving a proffered favour. In either case the necessity is equally absolute. Without the work of Christ there would be no salvation; and without faith there is no salvation. He that believeth on the Son hath everlasting life. He that believeth not, shall not see life, but the wrath of God abideth on him.[55]

---

55   Charles Hodge, *Systematic theology*. Originally published 1872 (Oak Harbor, WA: Logos Research Systems, Inc., 1997), 2:365.

One thing Hodge points out which is not precisely on point with the current argument is that this covenant is for adults. He says, "so far as adults are concerned," leaving the door open for children and infants to enter the covenant by other means if they are to be partakers at all in this covenant. This would appear to be a back door attempt to lay groundwork for an apologetic for baptizing infants. While erroneous, it speaks to the noble motivation of Covenantalists to account for the salvation of children. While incorrectly adduced, this indirectly underscores the point that the Covenant of Grace is only effective to those who express belief. Faith, therefore, is a crucial condition that must be satisfied to place one into the Covenant of Grace.

Paul P. Enns identifies one of the prevailing weaknesses in the Covenant of Grace as a complete answer to how God operates with mankind throughout the course of the Bible:

> The Covenant of Grace has an important emphasis in stressing the concept of grace in salvation. Probably the overriding weakness of the idea of this covenant is that it is an oversimplification; whereas it observes an abiding similarity in God's relationship to humanity, it fails to account for emphatic differences in that relationship. The Covenant of Grace is said to cover the time from Adam to the end of the age, with no distinctions being made between the differing covenants and covenanted people throughout this period. Scriptures related to Israel (e.g., Ezek. 36:25–28)) are made to refer to the Church. Other such areas of legitimate distinction need to be considered by Covenant theologians.[56]

---

56 Enns, 509.

The idea of distinctions in God's interaction with mankind is a strong point in favor of Dispensationalism. While the Covenant of Grace does an excellent job in explaining the unchanging nature of salvation, it fails to take into account the entirety of the biblical data. While the Covenant of Works had little support in Scripture, a clear teaching regarding the Covenant of Grace is completely absent. The fact that the New Covenant is often confused with the Covenant of Grace is evidence that perhaps a different name should have been chosen other than "covenant." As will be shown in the next chapter, Scripture is already teeming with explicit teachings about covenants, and a theological covenant not found in Scripture does nothing to decrease confusion. If the Covenant of Redemption can be demonstrated to be another derived "covenant," perhaps the best answer to harmonization would be for Covenant Theology to drop the "covenant" label and thereby provide less confusion to students of theology.

C. Covenant of Redemption (Eternal)

The Covenant of Redemption is inferred from Scripture, not specifically stated.[57] This is similar to the previous covenants examined, but the explicit references to the Covenant of Redemption coupled with the late development in its integration into the formulation of Covenant Theology suggests that implicit evidence is a few steps down on a derivation of doctrine flowchart. This does not make it unbiblical, but to apply the term "covenant" to this aspect of God's plan of redemption is more of a stretch than the Covenant of Grace. While terms such as the trinity are not explicit in Scripture, the evidence is lacking that a formal

---

57   Enns.

"covenant" ever took place among the Godhead and to speculate on the terms of such a covenant is similar to the conjectures required about logical order of eternal decrees.

Charles Hodge traces this doctrine through the time of Augustine:

> The Augustinian scheme includes the following points: (1.) That the glory of God, or the manifestation of his perfections, is the highest and ultimate end of all things. (2.) For that end God purposed the creation of the universe, and the whole plan of providence and redemption. (3.) That He placed man in a state of probation, making Adam, their first parent, their head and representative. (4.) That the fall of Adam brought all his posterity into a state of condemnation, sin, and misery, from which they are utterly unable to deliver themselves. (5.) From the mass of fallen men God elected a number innumerable to eternal life, and left the rest of mankind to the just recompense of their sins. (6.) That the ground of this election is not the foresight of anything in the one class to distinguish them favourably from the members of the other class, but the good pleasure of God. (7.) That for the salvation of those thus chosen to eternal life, God gave his own Son, to become man, and to obey and suffer for his people, thus making a full satisfaction for sin and bringing in everlasting righteousness, rendering the ultimate salvation of the elect absolutely certain. (8.) That while the Holy Spirit, in his common operations, is present with every man, so long as he lives, restraining evil and exciting good, his certainly efficacious and saving power is exercised only in behalf of the elect. (9.) That all those whom God has thus chosen to life, and for whom Christ specially

gave Himself in the Covenant of Redemption, shall certainly (unless they die in infancy), be brought to the knowledge of the truth, to the exercise of faith, and to perseverance in holy living unto the end.

Such is the great scheme of doctrine known in history as the Pauline, Augustinian, or Calvinistic, taught, as we believe, in the Scriptures, developed by Augustine, formally sanctioned by the Latin Church, adhered to by the witnesses of the truth during the Middle Ages, repudiated by the Church of Rome in the Council of Trent, revived in that Church by the Jansenists, adopted by all the Reformers, incorporated in the creeds of the Protestant Churches of Switzerland, of the Palatinate, of France, Holland, England, and Scotland, and unfolded in the Standards framed by the Westminster Assembly, the common representative of Presbyterians in Europe and America.

It is a historical fact that this scheme of doctrine has been the moving power in the Church; that largely to it are to be referred the intellectual vigour and spiritual life of the heroes and confessors who have been raised up in the course of ages; and that it has been the fruitful source of good works, of civil and religious liberty, and of human progress. Its truth may be evinced from many different sources.[58]

What this covenant does entail is the totality of God's plan of redemption that covers all of human history, both before the Fall and until Christ's second advent. William

---

58   Hodge, *Systematic Theology*, Originally Published 1872, 2:333-334.

Shedd merges all of Covenant Theology into just this one covenant, saying they are "two modes or phases of the one evangelical covenant of mercy."[59]

This statement is generally traced back to the Puritan author John Owen. His view is captured clearly in *The Works of John Owen,* where he states that the Covenant of Redemption pertains to a "dispensation of Christ's being punished for us, which also hath influence into his whole mediation on our behalf. This is that compact, covenant, convention, or agreement that was between the Father and the Son, for the accomplishment of the work of our redemption by the mediation of Christ, to the praise of the glorious grace of God."[60] Owens goes on to say, "The will of the Father appointing and designing the Son to be the head, husband, deliverer, and redeemer of His elect, His Church, His people, whom He did foreknow, with the will of the Son voluntarily, freely undertaking that work and all that was required thereunto, is that compact (for in that form it is proposed in the Scripture) that we treat of."[61] Here Owens references the eternal covenant and by this means the same as the Covenant of Redemption. Again, confusion may set in as the commonly understood "eternal covenant" is that of Ezekiel 16:60 where it is also known as an "everlasting covenant." The reference of Ezekiel is to the New Covenant and not what Owens means here. Again, the choice of terminology of covenants creates an unclear picture of the biblical teaching.

If any of the dispensations or covenants that have been named, shaped, discussed, analyzed, changed or invented

---

59   William G. T. Shedd, *Dogmatic Theology,* 3 vols., 2d ed. (Reprint. Nashville: Nelson, 1980), 2:360.

60   John Owen, *The Works of John Owen,* Volume 12 (London: Banner of Truth Trust, 1966), 496.

61   Ibid.

throughout the course of Church history, perhaps no other covenant explains the Bible better than the Covenant of Redemption, even if the term covenant is inadequate. The theme of the Bible beyond the glory of God is His plan of restoration and redemption that is offered through Jesus Christ.[62]

Osterhaven defines the Covenant of Redemption as follows:

> The Covenant of Redemption was made between God the Father and God the Son in eternity past in which they "covenanted together for the redemption of the human race, the Father appointing the Son to be the mediator; the Second Adam, whose life would be given for the salvation of the world, and the Son accepting the commission, promising that he would do the work which the Father had given him to do and fulfill all righteousness by obeying the law of God."[63]

The issue becomes whether or not when one defines the Covenant of Redemption they are in fact speaking of the Covenant of Grace. The aspects of each are startlingly similar. As has been shown, these two covenants are sometimes used interchangeably and little distinction if any is shown by Covenantalists. One could argue that the Covenant of Redemption is the only covenant that exists. The Covenant of Works was merely the required misstep of Adam that was needed for God to usher in His Covenant of Redemption announced in Genesis 3:15 and the rest of

---

62   See Goldsworthy and Edmund P. Clowney, *The Unfolding Mystery: Discovering Christ in the Old Testament* (Phillipsburgh, NJ: Presbyterian and Reformed, 1988).

63   M. E. Osterhaven, "Covenant Theology" in Walter A. Elwell, ed., *Evangelical Dictionary of Theology* (Grand Rapids: Baker, 1984), 280.

the Bible is exposition of the Covenant of Redemption that is termed the Covenant of Grace. But the order by which God has chosen to unfurl this plan into human history is as speculative as the lapsarian controversy mentioned above.

As this study of the three covenants has shown, an argument exists for the biblical data explicitly supporting but one of the three covenants and even the covenant explicitly mentioned, the Covenant of Works, is not universally agreed upon as being a reference to Adam in the Garden. The main point however, is that God has always had but one plan of salvation; there was never a Plan B. To use the term covenant in describing this branch of theology is confusing to the point of being unhelpful, even if the story of redemption is vital to the Bible and the truths for which the Reformers and modern day Covenantalists argue. One area where this becomes apparent is that Scripture does speak of redemption explicitly. For instance Berkhof notes, "There are numerous Scripture passages that emphasize the eternal nature of the plan of salvation (Eph. 1:3–14; 3:11; 2 Thessalonians 2:13; 2 Tim. 1:9; James 2:5; 1 Pet. 1:2). Moreover, Christ referred to His coming as a commissioning (John 5:30, 43; 6:38–40; 17:4–12). Christ is also regarded as the representative of the human race, the head of a covenant (Rom. 5:12–21; 1 Cor. 15:22)."[64] The inference of a covenant in Romans 5 may serve to bolster the argument that there is in fact a Covenant of Grace with Christ as its head, and the understanding of the similarities between Covenant Theology and Dispensationalism that are presented in this work would not be at odds with such a conclusion, but as the next chapter will demonstrate, there are plenty of uses for covenant that are clear and explicit throughout Scripture, and to create more covenants that are not explicit may do more harm than

---

64   Berkhof, 266.

good. On the other hand, "Plan of Redemption Theology" or some other moniker may add to the confusion should Covenantalists agree with the propositions here made.

One final note on the Covenant of Redemption is related to its derived nature. Is the covenant between the Father and the Son, or are all three members of the trinity included? Because of the lack of explicitness, most Covenantal theologians are not dogmatic on this nuanced point. Enns opts for the full trinity being a part, and will serve as a closing to this study of the Covenant of Redemption:

> In the eternal plan of God it was decreed that the Father would plan the redemption through election and predestination; the Son would provide redemption through His atoning death; the Holy Spirit would affect the plan through regenerating and sealing the believers (Eph. 1:3–14).

> The features of the Covenant of Redemption relate to the work assigned to the Son. To achieve the redemption of man, Christ had to take on humanity in a genuine incarnation (Rom. 8:3). As man's representative, Christ became the guarantee of a better covenant—one that could genuinely effect salvation (Heb. 7:22). Christ subjected Himself to the dictates of the law, perfectly fulfilling the requirements of the law so that He could redeem a humanity under bondage to the law (Gal. 4:4–5). Final release of bondage from enslavement to the law came through the atoning death of Christ (Gal. 3:13).[65]

---

65   Enns, 508.

CHAPTER 4

HOW MANY COVENANTS ARE IN THE BIBLE?

As discussed in the previous few chapters, the Covenantal theologian's understanding of the term covenant refers not to the biblical material per se, but instead refers to an overarching understanding of the covenants God makes with Adam and with each individual sinner who is covered by grace by accepting the shed blood of Christ as fulfillment of the penalty of sin for his or her life. So in essence this is not a covenant in the sense of either the Old Covenant known as the Old Testament or the New Covenant as inscripturated in the New Testament, neither is it the meta-Covenant of Redemption. Such covenantal terminology can lead to much confusion, especially the mixing of biblical covenants and theological covenants.

Therefore, an overview of the covenants that are in Scripture will be helpful to the harmonized understanding of covenants as they relate to Dispensationalism. This chapter will demonstrate that the introduction of a covenant does not indicate that a new "plan of salvation" is now in effect. Covenants and "plans of salvation" are never mixed in the Bible. One plan of salvation exists and has so since time began, and to name this plan a covenant, while perhaps not technically incorrect, leads to misunderstandings. The misunderstanding from a Dispensational perspective is because this plan Is not a series of dispensations where the method upon which man is saved differs depending on the relationship between God and man, and a misunderstanding of how the term covenant is used in Scripture. Further, as both sides would like to support their position with as much biblical evidence as available, an investigation of the covenants of Scripture will help the reader see how tangential the views of each side of the debate are when compared to the actual covenantal concepts in the Bible.

The first usage of the word covenant is in Genesis 6:18, "But I will establish My covenant with you, and you will enter the ark with your sons, your wife, and your sons' wives." Goldsworthy says of this covenant:

> The first reference to covenant, then, involves God's commitment to save Noah and his family from destruction. This salvation does not mean eternal life in itself, but we must say that it certainly points in that direction. Eternal life as it is spoken of in the New Testament is way over the horizon from the Old Testament's person's view. . . We are justified in referring to the first covenant statement as a covenant of salvation, even though the fuller meaning of salvation has yet to be revealed.[66]

---

66   Goldsworthy, 114.

Goldsworthy, like O. Palmer Robertson, attempts to see Christ and salvation in every covenant.[67] While the same stretching will be shown regarding testing, failure, and judgment when common themes are sought through each dispensation, some covenants require some special pleading to see salvation as the main theme. Nonetheless, deliverance is certainly a major motif of this first covenant. God spared Noah and his family, and promised never again to destroy the earth by a flood. But to say this covenant relates to Covenant Theology in any manner is not argued by Covenantal theologians. From Genesis 3:15 onward, which occurs chronologically prior to the flood, only one theological covenant has been in effect, regardless of the different aspects of the subsequent biblical covenants.

The Lord made two covenants with Abraham (Genesis 15 and 17), but they are actually just expansions of the initial promise (Genesis 12:27). The importance of this covenant even above the previous ones is related to the clearer salvific promises made, and the establishment of a "people of God." God promised Abraham many descendents. These descendents would one day possess the Promised Land for the entire duration of eternity; God will be their God; and through them all the nations of the world will be blessed.[68]

Israel as a nation appears to be who God has in mind as the "people of God." The question then becomes, after Christ comes and establishes His Church, does this nullify the Jews as God's chosen people? Apparently if that answer is yes, the Jews have lost their preferential status. God never intended to, nor did He save "All Israel" in the sense that He saved a person based on their ethnic background and not on their faith in God. Individuals among the community had to

---

67   See O. Palmer Robertson, *The Christ of the Covenants* (Phillips-burgh, NJ: Presbyterian and Reformed, 1981).

68   Goldsworthy, 121.

express faith in God, being a Jew did not automatically make one a redeemed citizen of the Kingdom. But these promises are beyond just salvation promises. As will be shown with other covenants, not every aspect of the covenant points to salvation. Possession of a land by lost persons must be granted as part of what God promises unless one is to argue that all Jews are redeemed.

Paul does not agree with this assessment, as Romans 11 points out, "I ask, then, has God rejected His people? Absolutely not! For I too am an Israelite, a descendent of Abraham, from the tribe of Benjamin. God has not rejected His people whom He foreknew. (Romans 11:1-2a)." Upon the initial granting of this covenant by God, Abraham's descendents became God's chosen people. And God has not rejected them. If God were using Israel as only a type, as an object lesson about faith, the Jews would have no hope of receiving the promises made to them as an ethnic group in the future, which would make Paul's statement contradictory. Changing the game midstream by applying spiritual meanings to literal promises does not appear to be consistent with God's promises. As Goldsworthy explains:

> God is not playing games with Israel for the sake of us who come afterward. His promises are true for them, and the way of salvation is made plain. Yet the failures of the saving figures, the prophets, the priests and the kings, as well as the overall failure of Israel, all point to the fact that the real saving event lies in the future.[69]

Paul assures the Romans that the covenant promises made to Israel have not been abrogated even if Christ has come and established His Church. It was for the benefit of

---

69   Goldsworthy, 161.

the Gentiles that God's chosen people, Israel, are currently experiencing a hardening and rejection of their Messiah (Romans 9:1-5; 11:25-27). God's promises will stand and are unchanging.[70] The Gentiles now have access to those same promises, and these are even mentioned in the covenant promises to Abraham, that all the nations would be blessed through Abraham. While a later chapter discusses the Israel/Church distinctions, of importance here to note is the blessings to all Nations (i.e. Gentiles) are clearly stated in this covenant. This covenant was subsequently renewed to Isaac (Genesis 26) and to Jacob (Genesis 28).

So what promises and predictions did God make to national Israel and to Abraham that have not been fulfilled? John Walvoord states:

> In summary, the Scriptures predicted that Abraham's people would leave the land promised to them, and that was literally fulfilled in their bondage in Egypt. It was also predicted that they would come back to the literal land, and they did. The Assyrian and Babylonian captivities were predicted, and they were literally fulfilled. It was predicted that Israel would come back to the land, and this again was literally fulfilled.

> Subsequent to the life, death, and resurrection of Christ, Jerusalem was destroyed in A.D. 70, and the people of Israel were indeed scattered throughout the whole world. All of this illustrated and supports the pattern of literal fulfillment in relation to a literal land for a literal nation Israel. The only real question which remains is whether the Bible predicts that

---

70   Richard Longenecker, "Galatians," *Word Biblical Commentary*, Volume 41 (Waco, TX: Word, 1990), 128-130.

they will come back to the land for a third time and possess it forever.[71]

The answer to this question proposed by Walvoord is answered by the prophet Jeremiah:

> However, take note! The days are coming"—the Lord's declaration—"when it will no longer be said: As the Lord lives who brought the Israelites from the land of Egypt, 15 but rather: As the Lord lives who brought the Israelites from the land of the north and from all the other lands where He had banished them. For I will return them to their land that I gave to their ancestors.

> "I am about to send for many fishermen"—the Lord's declaration—"and they will fish for them. Then I will send for many hunters, and they will hunt them down on every mountain and hill and out of the clefts of the rocks (Jeremiah 16:14-16)

The obvious conclusion is that the previous promises were literally fulfilled, so the prophecy of Jeremiah should be fulfilled in the Millennial Kingdom. A great mistake is made when one understands the promises made to Abraham as the being completely fulfilled in the Old Covenant. While the Old Covenant is done away with and no longer in force, that does not mean everything promised to Abraham is now transferred to Christ. Hebrews points out clearly that the Old Covenant is the Law given at Sinai. Perhaps many problems Covenantalists have with Dispensationalists would be cleared up if the teaching about the promises to Abraham and Israel were more emphatic when stressing that the Abrahamic

---

71   John F. Walvoord, "Does the Church Fulfill Israel's Program? – Part 1," *Bibliotheca Sacra* (Dallas, TX: Dallas Theological Seminary, 1996).

Covenant is not the same as the Old Covenant. To clarify terminology and help others understand Dispensationalism, it is perhaps better to think of the promises to Abraham as promises that God has partially fulfilled and will ultimately fulfill rather than as the Abrahamic covenant. Although it is true that it is a covenant, to confuse this covenant with the Mosaic covenant could set a person on his or her way towards Replacement Theology and miss the purposes that remain for Israel in the Millennial Kingdom.

The third covenant mentioned in Scripture is this very Mosaic covenant made with the nation of Israel at Sinai. The terms of this covenant follow closely with the *suzerainty* treaty described in chapter 1. This covenant is tied to the Abrahamic covenant and carries the progressive revelation a lot further along in regards to making known such things as atonement, sacrifice, and godly living, but this was always meant to be a temporary covenant. A later chapter will show this as a parenthesis in the overall promise of salvation, but pregnant with types and shadows of the Messiah that is to come and fulfill the Law given to Moses.

This covenant came after the suffering of God's people in Egypt. God, always faithful to His promises, leads His people out of Egypt and into the Promised Land. This covenant was given at Sinai and is rightly described as the Old Covenant. The Law served a purpose, as a pedagogue or schoolmaster, but it was also a prison, showing how man does not meet God's requirements. Certain types and shadows existed that relate to the Age of Grace, and the sacrificial system points toward a sacrifice suitable for propitiation in God's sight, but Chapter 10 will elaborate on the necessity for the Christian who lives now in the Age of Grace not to attempt meeting the civil and ceremonial aspects of the Law.

The Mosaic covenant is referenced and renewed many times throughout the Old Testament. At Schechem, the covenant is renewed by Joshua (Joshua 8:30-35; Deuteronomy 7:1-8)[72] After recounting once again how gracious God had been in fulfilling His promises, he calls upon Israel to renew and keep the covenant, setting up a stone as a witness (Joshua 24:16-27).[73]

A recurring theme in renewing the covenant made with Israel is fourfold. A review of the history of Israel, a call upon the people to obey the covenant, warning of the consequences of disobedience, and a response by the people that they acknowledge they have failed to live up to their part of the covenant.[74] Usually a reassurance that the Lord will not forsake His people is included as well. Therefore, the renewal by Samuel would qualify as covenant renewal, even if the word is not found in 1 Samuel 12. The elements are present: the history of Israel is reviewed (12:8-13), Samuel calls on the people to obey the terms of the covenant (12:14, 20-21), Samuel issues a warning about the consequences of disobedience (12:15, 25), a response by Israel acknowledging their unfaithfulness to the covenant, and finally a reassurance that the Lord will not abandon them (12:22).[75]

Another such allusion to covenant renewal is in 1 Kings 18. This is the scene where Elijah and the prophets of Baal and Asherah come together to see which God is the true God.[76] Bradshaw finds many allusions in this scene to the Mosaic covenant:

> The episode has clear allusions to a covenant renewal, while Elijah is portrayed as a type of Moses. The construction of the altar from 12 stones,

---

72   Bradshaw.
73   Ibid.
74   Ibid.
75   Ibid.
76   Ibid.

representing the 12 tribes (18:31) recalling both the events at Sinai (Exodus 24:4) and the command to Joshua at the time of Conquest (Josh. 4:8-9, 20). The people respond to the fire from heaven by affirming that the Lord was God (1 Kings 18:39). In the next chapter the Elijah-Moses parallel becomes clear when Elijah flees to Mt. Horeb (Sinai of the Exodus), a journey of 40 days (Exodus. 24:18; 34:28). There Elijah complains of how the Israelites have rejected his Covenant (1 Kings 19:10) and calls for His judgment upon them (cf. Exodus. 32:11-13). The Lord's response is not to answer by either wind, earthquake or fire (Exodus. 19:16-19), but in a "still small voice". The covenant breakers would be punished according to the terms of the Mosaic Covenant - by the sword (Lev. 26:25) - specifically by the swords of Hazael and Jehu (1 Kings 19:17). The continuance of the Covenant is assured by the presence of a godly remnant in the land (1 Kings 19:18; Rom. 11:2-5).[77]

Other instances of renewal of this covenant are by Jehoida and Joash (2 Kings 11:17-18)[78], Hezekiah (1 Chronicles 29-30), [79] Josiah (2nd Chronicles 34-35),[80] and Ezra/Nehemiah (Nehemiah 9:5-37; 10:32-39).[81]

Before moving on to the New Covenant, there are two other covenants instituted by God and given to man in the Old Testament. The first of which is a promise made to Phineas, the son of Eleazar, the son of Aaron. In Numbers

---

77   Ibid.
78   Ibid.
79   Ibid.
80   Ibid.
81   Ibid.

25, while Israel was at Acacia Grove, the Moabite women not only had sexual relations with the Israelites, but also encouraged the worship of foreign gods. So great was this transgression that Phineas took a spear and killed an Israelite man and a Moabite woman who were engaged in the act of ritual prostitution in the Tent of Meeting (Numbers 25:6-8).[82] Because of Phineas' zeal for the Lord, God made a covenant of peace with him and established an everlasting priesthood for Phineas and his descendents. This line of Phineas served as high priest through the time of Eli and his sons (from Ithamar according to 1 Chronicles 24:3).[83] A break in the line then occurred (1 Samuel 1-3), but God did not forget His covenant with Phineas, and when the Tabernacle and priesthood was restored by David he selected a descendent of Phineas, Zadok, to serve as the high priest. This line continued until 171 BC when Antiochus IV removed the priesthood from Jason to Menelaus (2 Maccabees 4:23).[84]

The covenant between God and David is a subset of the New Covenant, but because of its individual nature and Messianic overtones, it does not quite fit as a part of the New Covenant; a covenant made with the house of Israel and the house of Judah. Bradshaw describes this covenant between God and David:

> In response to David's expressed desire to build a temple for the Lord in Jerusalem the Lord spoke through the prophet Nathan. David was not the one to build a temple, rather the Lord would establish a house for David and his kingdom would last forever (2 Sam. 7:12-17). Although this passage does not

82 Ibid.
83 Ibid.
84 F.F. Bruce, *New Testament History* (London: Doubleday, 1969), 58.

use the word covenant at all the word is connected with the same incident elsewhere in Scripture (2 Sam. 23:2-7; Psalm 89:3-4, 27-28). The promise was seen as the renewal of the promises made to Abraham to a specific family, as the wording of Psalm 72:17 makes clear (cf. Gen. 12:3). These promises led to several developments in Hebrew theology. **a) The City of God.** David's city, located on Mount Zion became the focus of soteriological and eschatological interest, rather than the whole of the Promised Land (Psalm 48:2; 133:3; Isaiah 2:2-4; 51:3; Micah 4:1-4; cf. Heb. 12:22; 13:14; Rev. 21). It also led to the belief that Jerusalem would never fall (Isaiah 33:20-22; Jeremiah 26:1-19), a belief shattered by the conquest by Nebuchadnezzar of Babylon (Psalm 137:1-3; Micah 3:9-12). **b) The Messiah.** The idea of an ideal Davidite is developed in the Psalms and the prophetic writings. This "anointed one" or "Messiah" would rule the nations from Zion and serve as a priest after the order of Melchizedek (Psalm 2; 110). Like his forefather he would be born in Bethlehem in Judah (Micah 5:2; cf. Matt. 2:1-6). The Lord would chastise him for sin, and there remained the possibility that part of the Davidic line would be excluded because of sin, as happened in the case of Jehoikim (cf. Jer. 22:18-30). Nevertheless, the promise would be fulfilled (Jer. 23:5-6). The writers of the Gospels demonstrated clearly that these prophecies were fulfilled in the life and ministry of Jesus (Matt. 1:1; 9:27; 12:23; 22:21-46; Luke 1:32, 68-69; 20:41-44; Acts 2:25-31).[85]

---

85   Bradshaw.

The New Covenant does not start in the New Testament, but is present in the Old. The only reference to the "New Covenant" in the Old Testament is in Jeremiah 31:31. It is clear from the reference that this covenant replaces the Old Covenant which Israel broke. This covenant includes all of the constituent parts of the preceding covenants and fulfills and achieves the purposes of the Noahic, Abrahamic, Mosaic and Davidic (cf. Ezekiel 16:60-63).[86] The covenant is "made with the reconstituted people of Israel and Judah (31:31; 33:14). These people will be ruled by a descendent of David (33:15-19) and ministered to by the Levites (33:18-22), promises as sure and binding and the covenant with creation (31:35-37; 33:19-26; cf. Gen. 8:22)."[87]

The New Covenant is mentioned in all of the synoptic gospels and is clearly associated with the shed blood of Jesus Christ. (see Matthew 26:28; Mark 14:24; Luke 22:20; cf. 1 Cor. 11:25) where Jesus points to His own death and shed blood in an allusion to Moses in Exodus 24:7.[88]

Paul makes it clear that the covenant promises to Israel remain. Bradshaw writes of the hardening passages by Paul as thus:

> In Romans Paul maintains that the covenant promises made to Israel have not been forgotten. Rather, Israel experienced a hardening for the benefit of the Gentiles (Rom. 9:1-5; 11:25-27) who had now been allowed access to benefits of the promises (Eph. 2:11-13). The New and the Mosaic (old) covenants are contrasted in much the same way by Paul as they were by Jeremiah; the old is of the letter and brought condemnation while the New

---

86   Ibid.
87   Ibid.
88   Ibid.

is of the Spirit and brings righteousness (2 Cor. 3:4-18; Gal. 4:21-31).[89]

In Hebrews 8-10, the New Covenant is clearly contrasted with the Mosaic covenant (see Table 1 below).

Table 1: The Contrast Between Old & New Covenants According to the Writer to the Hebrews[90]

Old Covenant	New Covenant
Earthly (9:1)	Heavenly (8:1-2)
Copy and a shadow (8:5; 9:23; 10:1)	Real and true (8:2; 9:24 10:1)
Mortal human priests (7:23)	Immortal High Priest (7:24)
Regulated by the Law (8:4)	Divinely administered (8:1-2)
Administered by sinful priests (9:7)	Administered by a sinless High Priest (4:15)
Sacrifices constantly repeated (9:6-7, 25; 10:11)	One sacrifice carried out once for all time (9:12, 26; 10:10, 12)
Offered the blood of animals (9:18-22)	Jesus offered his own blood (9:12, 26)
Limited efficacy (10:1-4)	Eternal efficacy (10:12)
No inner cleansing achieved (9:9)	Leads to sanctification and a cleansed conscience (9:14; 10:14)

This survey of the Old and New Covenants, the promises to Abraham, the covenants with Phineas and with David does not exhaust the biblical repository of covenant dealings. Those discussed deal with God's initiative in establishing covenants with man and with creation. A covenant in the Bible could also include other parties involved in covenant with one another.

The covenant of marriage is the first covenant referred to in the Bible (Genesis 2:22-24).[91] This would fall under

---

89   Ibid.

90   C.C. Newman, "Covenant, New Covenant," Ralph P. Martin & Peter H. Davids, *Dictionary of the Later New Testament* (Leicester: IVP, 1997), 248. This table is based on Newman's work as created by Bradshaw in "Covenant."

91   Ibid.

the category of a *parity* treaty as opposed to a *suzerainty* treaty. Also, another covenant is made between the spies in Jericho with Rahab after she supplies protection for them. The stipulations on the part of the spies are to spare her and anyone in her home's lives if she identifies the house that belongs to her with a scarlet cord during the attack on Jericho (Joshua 2:8-14; 6:22-23).[92] Other covenants found in the Old Testament between people include David and Jonathan (1 Samuel 18:1-4; 2 Samuel 1:26), David and Abner (2 Samuel 3:12-13), and Solomon and Simei (1 Kings 2:42-46).[93]

Covenants were not limited to individual parties, but also nations entered into covenant with one another as well as individuals with other nations. One such example is that of Abraham and the Amorites in Genesis 14:13. Abraham makes a covenant as well with the king of Gerar, Abimelech in Genesis 21:22-32). This covenant was renewed by Abraham's son Isaac in Genesis 26:26-31.[94] A covenant of deception was entered into by Joshua with the Gibeonites, and even though it was made deceptively it was binding (Joshua 9:3-27). When Saul broke this covenant (2 Samuel 21:1-3) the Lord punished Israel with a famine. Other such covenants include the covenant between the people of Jabesh Gilead & Nahash the Ammonite (1 Samuel 11:1-2), David and the nations he captured (2 Samuel 8:-14), followed by Solomon and the vassal states he demanded tribute from (1 Kings 4:21), and the parity treaty between Solomon and Hiram of Tyre, where Hiram established peace with David and Solomon (2 Samuel 5:11; 1 Kings 5:1-2) in exchange for timber and gold.[95] Between a king and his people covenants such as ones between David and Israel (2 Samuel 5:1-3),

---

92   Ibid.
93   Ibid.
94   Ibid.
95   Ibid.

Jehoida and the king's guards (2 Kings 11:4-8), Joash and Judah (2 Kings 11:17, and Zedekiah and Judah (Jeremiah 34:8-11) are found in Scripture.

Covenants are not limited to humans either in Scripture. In Job references can be found to covenants with stones (Job 5:23), with Job's own eyes (31:1), and with a Leviathan (41:4). Wild animals are brought into a covenant found in Hosea 2:18. A significant element of covenant curses involve threats by wild animals and Israel is promised that in the age to come these threats will be removed (cf. Ezekiel 34:25)[96]

In addition, allusions to covenants with the following can also be found: with death (Isaiah 28:15-19); with the day and the night (Jeremiah 33:19-26); with the Nations not to destroy Israel (Zechariah 11:10-11);[97] and with salt (Numbers 18:19; 2 Chronicles 13:5).[98]

What this survey of the covenants of Scripture has done for the reader is demonstrate that the term covenant and its various connotations and denotations in Scripture are not as cut and dried and easily understood as some may have thought. To say Covenant Theology is a belief in the various covenants of God is too simplistic, and ignores too much of the rich meanings and symbolism this term is used for when applied in different ways throughout Scripture. If, as the Covenantalists would argue, God has always only had "one" covenant people, than what relationship do these covenants have with this "one" group of people? To answer the question biblically is difficult, because the material in the Bible concerning covenants is not given in such a way as to

---

96   Douglas Stewart.

97   C.F. Keil and F. Delitzsch, "Minor Prophets," *Commentary on the Old Testament in Ten Volumes*, Vol. 10 (Grand Rapids, MI: Eerdmans, 1988). These verses are extremely obscure, and no other mention of this covenant is present in Scripture.

98   Bradshaw.

continually reaffirm and reestablish one overriding covenant. Perhaps a better understanding of this "one" people of God is to say that God has always had "one" plan of salvation, and everyone who is redeemed by God who is destined for eternal life is a member of this "one" covenant community, but to tie the covenant part of this term to the biblical material is conjectural and asks the text to do things for which it was not intended. Whether it be faithful and believing Israelites, Church members in Antioch, or Noah and his family, there is "one" people of God in the sense that God's grace has reached into history to redeem those whom He has chosen to redeem, but there are multifaceted ways in which God has dealt with His people in different epochs of time.

Therefore, Covenant Theology is deficient in understanding these various relationships, even if much is to be gained by a proper understanding of covenants in the Bible and God's plan of redemption that was worked out by God before human history began. The next part of this work will examine Dispensationalism to see if it can fill in the picture of God's dealings with mankind.

On the other hand, one can not look at each New Covenant as the ushering in of a new dispensation. Where would the covenant made with Phineas fit into this schema? And what of the covenant promises to David? These are to be fulfilled simultaneously with other covenants in a future dispensation. No magic bullet exists nor is there a bright line test that can be used to gauge or otherwise mark the dispensational changes that emerge from the covenant aspect of the Bible. Perhaps the best method of understanding biblical covenants is to not force them to agree to Covenant Theology or to Dispensationalism, but to let them speak for themselves as different covenants God made at different times to different people for different purposes that all work together for His glory.

PART II.
DISPENSATIONALISM

CHAPTER 5

INTRODUCTION TO DISPENSATIONALISM

The term "dispensation," like the term "covenant" is a word that appears in the Bible. And in a similar fashion as Covenant Theology, the system of interpretation known as "Dispensationalism" does not rest on the definition as found in Scripture. In other words, each time the word is found, there is not necessarily a change in dispensations. Wiersbe defines the word sometimes translated dispensation as follows:

> English word "economy" is derived directly from the Greek *oikonomia*, "the law of the house," or "a stewardship, a management." God has different ways of managing His program from age to age, and these different "stewardships" Bible students sometimes call "dispensations" (Eph. 1:9–10). God's principles do not change, but His methods of dealing with mankind do change over the course of

history. "Distinguish the ages," wrote St. Augustine, "and the Scriptures harmonize."[99]

When applied to the system of interpretation, the term takes on additional meaning, as does the term covenant when applied to Covenant Theology.

Dispensationalism tends to be a difficult theology to pin down and identify exactly what it is or what would qualify a person as a Dispensationalist. Paul S. Karleen introduces the topic with a series of questions and accusations commonly lobbed at those who claim the name Dispensationalist:

> If one mentions the word *Dispensationalism* in any group of evangelicals, there are likely to be various responses. What is a Dispensationalist? How can you recognize one? Is it a person who frequently attends Bible conferences? Once he is identified, can he be labeled immediately as unscholarly, as some might do?

> For some, Dispensationalism is foolishness. But for others it is a tremendous help in understanding the Bible. This writer believes it is a valid approach, and this section will provide a number of reasons in support of its accuracy and value.

> …We stress that the best system of interpretation is the one that opens up the most Scripture and allows Scripture to be consistent with itself. This type of interpretation is at the heart of Dispensationalism. It is really an approach to the Bible, rather than a system of theology. True enough, it includes certain truths regarding the Church, prophecy, and Israel,

99   W. W. Wiersbe, *The Bible Exposition Commentary* (Wheaton, IL: Victor Books, 1996), Eph 3:1.

but it is basically an outlook on the Bible that works on the basis of historic, orthodox tenets of the faith, and attempts to allow the Bible to open itself to the reader. This is clearly the factor that divides it from other conservative systems of interpretation. [100]

Within Covenant Theology, perhaps the greatest differences among its adherents would be in the numbering of the covenants, whether there be two or three, or perhaps whether the Covenant of Grace is distinct from the Covenant of Redemption, as well as speculation of how many members of the trinity are involved in the Covenant of Redemption. While significantly more detailed nuances do exist within Covenant Theology than just those, when compared to the diversity of beliefs held by those who claim to be Dispensationalists, these disagreements are minor. Perhaps the greatest lack of unanimity in Dispensationalism is determining just how many dispensations are presented in Scripture. While Covenant theologians debate whether or not there are one, two, or three covenants encompassing history, for Dispensationalists, it sometimes appears that any two Dispensationalists will either lack agreement on the overall number and certainly how they should be named! But whether or not this is of critical importance or not and whether this should cause one to disregard the theological system will have to be explored as well.

Before reviewing the dispensations, whatever their number may be, a brief sketch of the development and history will be undertaken. As Ryrie has stated, "Like all doctrines, dispensational teaching has undergone systematization and development in its lifetime, though the basic tenets have not

---

100 Karleen.

changed."[101] Therefore a survey of dispensational thought will be undertaken, with attention given to dispensational tendencies that emerged even prior to a formalized system known as Dispensationalism.

---

101 Ryrie, 13.

CHAPTER 6

HISTORY OF DISPENSATIONALISM

Charles Ryrie summarizes well in his book *Dispensationalism* the history of Christian thought that has led to the system known as Dispensationalism. He states:

> Dispensationalists recognize that as a *system* of theology it [Dispensationalism] is recent in origin. But there are historical references to that which eventually was systematized into Dispensationalism. There is evidence in the writings of men who lived long before Darby that the dispensational concept was part of their viewpoint.[102]

Thomas Ice acknowledges that Darby is rightly credited with the modern forms of Dispensationalism, but points as well to the historical foundations:

> The first systematic expression of Dispensationalism was formulated by J. N. Darby sometime during the late 1820s and 1830s in the British Isles. I believe

---

102 Ryrie, 71.

that Darby's development was the culmination of various influences which produced within his thought one of the most literal approaches to Bible interpretation in history and a theology which distinguishes God's plan for Israel from God's plan for the Church. . .

. . .Although Darby was the first to systematize Dispensationalism, I believe that rudimentary features can be found prior to the nineteenth century, especially in the early Church and the three hundred years prior to Darby. Opponents often debate a pre-Darby heritage, but I think the evidence does support our claim that there are historical and theological antecedents to the modern system.[103]

Ice notes many such antecedents reaching as far back into Church history as the ante-Nicene fathers such as "Justin Martyr (110-165), Irenaeus (130-200), Tertullian (c. 160-220), Methodius (d. 311), and Victorinus of Petau (d. 304)."[104]

Ice quotes Larry Crutchfield's summary of the early Church Fathers:

Regardless of the number of economies to which the Fathers held, the fact remains that they set forth what can only be considered a doctrine of ages and dispensations which foreshadows Dispensationalism as it is held today. Their views were certainly less well defined and less sophisticated. But it is evident that the early Fathers viewed God's dealings with His

103 Thomas Ice, "A Short History of Dispensationalism" (http://www.pre-trib.org/articles/view/short-history-of-Dispensationalism), [accessed 1/14/2010].
104 Ibid.

people in dispensational terms. . . . In every major area of importance in the early Church one finds rudimentary features of Dispensationalism that bear a striking resemblance to their contemporary offspring.[105]

Often thought of as a modern invention of Dispensationalists, Crutchfield explains that the distinctions between national Israel and the Church is not a modern idea, but is present throughout Church history:

The Fathers (1) distinguished between the Church and national Israel, (2) recognized distinctions among the differing peoples of God throughout biblical history, and (3) believed in the literal fulfillment of covenant promises in the earthly kingdom. . . . The contemporary dispensational position on Israel and the Church is primarily a refinement and not a contradiction of the position of the ante-Nicene Church.[106]

Ice says of the following period, "The Middle Ages were a time in which Premillennialism, literal interpretation, dispensations, and an Israel-Church distinction were largely absent from theological discussion or went underground.[107] Ice says of the Reformation:

The Reformation and post-Reformation periods did much to restore a more intensive study of the Bible to the Church. For the first time ever, printing made literature accessible to most anyone. A greater effort was also put forth to systemize the Bible

---

105 Larry Crutchfield, "Ages and Dispensations in the Ante-Nicene Fathers" *Bibliotheca Sacra* (October-December 1987). Quoted in Ice.

106 Ibid., 271. Quoted in Ice.

107 Ice.

within the light of Protestant theology. About 250 years before Darby, Reformed scholars developed a school of theology that is known as "Covenant Theology." With it, a precedent was established for viewing theology from the perspective of an important concept like "covenant." While others, like Jonathan Edwards (1703-58), wrote his "History of the Work of Redemption," which viewed God's salvation of man progressively in history. Such developments were preparing for the birth of modern Dispensationalism.[108]

As early as 1687, scholars such as Pierre Poiret were dividing the Scriptures into economies or dispensations. Charles Ryrie shows this by highlighting the crude, but systematized dispensational schema of Poiret in his six volume work, *The Divine Economy*:

I.   Infancy – to the Deluge
II.   Childhood – to Moses
III. Adolescence – to the prophets
IV. Youth – to the coming of Christ
V.   Manhood – "some time after that"
VI. Old Age – "the time of man's decay"
(V & VI are the Church Age)
VII. Renovation of all things – the Millennium[109]

Another famous theologian who is better known as a hymn writer, Isaac Watts (1674-1748), also was a pre-Darbyian Dispensationalist. He wrote a forty-page essay called "The Harmony of all the Religions which God ever Prescribed to Men and all His Dispensations towards

---

108 Ibid.
109 Ryrie, 71. Quoted in Ice.

them."[110] His dispensational scheme is even more developed than Poiret's:

I.   The Dispensation of Innocency
II. Adam after the Fall
III. The Noahic Dispensation
IV. The Abrahamic Dispensation
V.   The Mosaic Dispensation
VI. The Christian Dispensation[111]

Despite these pre-Darbyian articulations of Dispensationalism, the commonly accepted founder of the modern day system of Dispensationalism is John Nelson Darby. He rejected the "historicist" viewpoint of eschatology that was popular in British Millennialism. Since the time of Augustine Amillennialism was the predominant view of Revelation 20 and Premillennialism was in decline. Darby saw what the early Fathers saw when he read Revelation unclouded by centuries of perpetuated allegorical theology. He became a "futurist" who contributed greatly to the thinking of the Plymouth Brethren of whom he was a leader.[112] The two contributions Darby is most known for in bringing forward the idea of Dispensationalism is that the Church Age was a "parenthesis" or "intercalation" between the 69th and 70th "weeks" of years in Daniel 9:27-27 and that there would be a Rapture (based on 1 Thessalonians 4:17) whereby the Church would be removed to heaven during the 70th week of Daniel 9, or the "great tribulation."[113] These two ideas were certainly new to the study of the Bible and to Christianity. It is from these beginnings that

---

110 Ice.

111 Ryrie, 73. Quoted in Ice.

112 E. Fahlbusch and G.W. Bromiley, *The Encyclopedia of Christianity* (Grand Rapids: Eerdmans, 2003), 1:854.

113 Ibid.

the divide between Israel and the Church initially began to reach the levels where theology stands today. And as will be demonstrated, the divide between these two has become a pivotal issue in debate among Dispensationalists and nondispensationalists.

The next major movement in Dispensationalism occurred upon the publication of the *Scofield Study Bible*. The first record of Dispensationalism in America was when John Nelson Darby twice visited the U.S. in 1864-1865. It was during these two visits that a Presbyterian pastor named Dr. James H. Brooks came under conviction that Dispensationalism was proper understanding of Scripture.[114] One of Dr. Brooks' students was Cyrus Ingerson Scofield.

Scofield was originally a lawyer, and grew up near Lebanon, TN. Ordained as a Congregational minister in 1882; he was a staunch supporter of Dispensationalism. His first dispensational book was entitled *Rightly Dividing the Word of Truth*, published in 1907. After garnering financial assistance, he produced the *Scofield Bible* which drew mixed reactions. Critics began what has now become a continual criticism of Dispensationalism, by claiming that Scofield's approach to Christ's return had replaced the cross of Christ as the central point of history.[115] As will be demonstrated later, this is a spurious claim of Scofield and Dispensationalism as a whole, as salvation has always been based on the crucifixion under any orthodox Christian teaching. Dispensationalism boasts as high a Christology as the Christology of Covenant Theology. The broadened teachings of the end time events and of Israel do nothing to diminish the work of Christ or

---

114 Ernest Reisinger, "A History of Dispensationalism in America," *The Founders Journal* January/February 2009.

115 J.D. Douglas, P.W. Comfort and D. Mitchell, eds. *Who's Who in Christian History* (Wheaton, IL: Tyndale House, 1997).

the cross event. Scofield's Bible became and still is one of the best selling study Bibles of all time.

Besides Charles Ryrie's *Dispensationalism*, which is one of the best known defenses of Dispensationalism, these two men set the stage and most clearly defined classical Dispensationalism. Paul P. Enns summarizes the events after Scofield which bring Dispensationalism to present:

> The writings of Dallas Theological Seminary professors have promulgated Dispensationalism in recent years. Charles Ryrie's *Dispensationalism Today* is undoubtedly the premier defense of Dispensationalism. Other writings, such as J. Dwight Pentecost's *Things to Come* and the eschatological writings of John F. Walvoord (principally *The Millennial Kingdom* and the trilogy *Israel in Prophecy, The Church in Prophecy,* and *The Nations in Prophecy*) have ably set forth the dispensational position. Charles L. Feinberg's *Millennialism: Two Major Views* has equally defended this system. Lewis Sperry Chafer's august *Systematic Theology* sets forth Dispensationalism in a comprehensive manner.
>
> Among the schools that are avowedly dispensational are: Dallas Theological Seminary, Grace Theological Seminary, Talbot Theological Seminary, Western Conservative Baptist Seminary, Multnomah School of the Bible, Moody Bible Institute, Philadelphia College of the Bible, and many others.[116]

One Dispensational school among these mentioned by Enns is worthy of additional comment. The reason for mentioning this branch of Dispensationalism is due

---

116 Enns, 517.

to the fact that more traditional Dispensationalists often distance themselves from it. Dallas Theological seminary has fostered a type of Dispensationalism quite different from the classical view, but not fully disconnected from the idea of dispensations.

Progressive Dispensationalism finds its roots in 1985, when twenty four Dispensationalists met at Biola University and started the Dispensational Study Group to discuss and study Dispensationalism. The group meets regularly at the annual meetings of the Evangelical Theological Society.[117] Of the movement Blaising writes:

> Progressive Dispensationalism offers a number of modifications to classical and revised Dispensationalism which brings Dispensationalism closer to contemporary evangelical biblical interpretation. Although the name is relatively recent, the particular interpretations that make up this form of Dispensationalism have been developing over the past fifteen years. Sufficient revisions had taken place by 1991 to introduce the name Progressive Dispensationalism at the national meeting of the Evangelical Theology Society that year.[118]

Not all Dispensationalists would treat this as a legitimate subset of the dispensational movement. Charles Ryrie considers what the differences between normative Dispensationalism and Progressive Dispensationalism entail:

> The crucial consideration is not that there are some differences, but what those differences are.

---

117 "Charting Dispensationalism" *Christianity Today* (September 12, 1994): 26.

118 Blaising and Bock, *Dispensationalism*, 22-3.

Are they minor or major? In general, differences in interpretations and emphases among normative Dispensationalists do not change the overall system of Dispensationalism, whereas the differences advanced by progressive Dispensationalists do form a new and revised system that some (both Dispensationalists and nondispensationalists) believe is not Dispensationalism anymore.[119]

So what differences advanced by Progressive Dispensationalism separate it from Normative or Classical Dispensationalism? One such distinctive noted by Ryrie is: "Progressive Dispensationalism advocates a *holistic* and *unified* view of eternal salvation."[120] This means that all the redeemed will be blessed with the same salvation with respect to justification and sanctification. One wonders if this is not similar to the concept and purpose of the Covenant of Grace in Covenant Theology.[121]

While this chapter is not intended to be a commentary or critique of the principles of Dispensationalism, the chapter would be deficient if something was not said about Ryrie's implications. The concept Blaising and Bock put forth is consistent with the principles of both Dispensationalism, which has the shed blood of Jesus Christ as the only satisfactory sacrifice for sin, Ryrie's response appears to be dismissive of such a statement. The fact that God has a plan for national Israel that differs from the Church takes nothing away from the fact that all who come to Christ are justified by His blood. The question would need to be asked of Ryrie,

---

119 Ryrie, *190*-191.
120 Blaising and Bock, 47. Quoted in Ibid., 191.
121 Ibid., 191.

"What other means could there be that the redeemed will be blessed with respect to justification and sanctification?" This is illustrative of some of the issues that remain with normative Dispensationalism in misunderstanding the true teaching of the Bible, and that of Covenantalists and Progressive Dispensationalists.

Before moving on, one additional problem Ryrie has with Progressive Dispensationalism must be evaluated. He critiques the dispensational scheme of Progressive Dispensationalism in terms of lumping two or more stewardships into one. For example, of the first dispensation (Patriarchal) recognized by Progressive Dispensationalists, he states:

> Progressive Dispensationalism charts four primary dispensations.[122] The first is the Patriarchal (from creation to Sinai). Although they acknowledge that other Dispensationalists see distinct dispensations within this broad period, it seems odd not to distinguish the pre-Fall arrangements God made with Adam and Eve as a separate dispensation. By every measurement this was a different stewardship. Furthermore, it seems necessary to distinguish the arrangement God introduced with Abraham in view of Paul's emphasis on the Abrahamic promises (Gal. 3:8-16) and in view of revisionists' own emphasis on the Abrahamic covenant. To lump pre-Fall conditions, post-Fall conditions, and the Abrahamic covenant under a common stewardship arrangement or dispensation is artificial, to say the least.[123]

---

122 Blaising and Bock, 123 as quoted in Ryrie 195.
123 Ryrie, 195.

This is an odd criticism of Progressive Dispensationalism in light of what will be shown to be a commonly accepted view concerning the number of dispensations. To state that the number of dispensations is now an important and indispensable aspect of Dispensationalism is a contradiction to Ryrie's own *Sine Qua Non* and goes against his own assertion that the exact number is not an imperative to make one an orthodox Dispensationalist. These statements are not meant to disparage Ryrie, but merely to point out that Covenant theologians are not the only ones who unfairly castigate those whose views differ from their own, even among those inside their camp committed to the foundational views of their hermeneutical perspective.

Based on these principles of Progressive Dispensationalism, it might be said that Progressive Dispensationalism is on the road towards Covenant Theology. The future of Progressive Dispensationalism will need to be monitored to see how close such views come to obliterating the distinctions essential to Dispensationalism so as to make it completely unrecognizable and unworthy of being under the umbrella of Dispensationalism. However, if an attempt to harmonize Covenant Theology with Dispensationalism has ever had inklings of success, it is that of Progressive Dispensationalism.

This brief survey of the history of Dispensationalism sets the stage for a discussion of the main tenets of Dispensationalism and to a discussion of how many different dispensations there have been or will be.

CHAPTER 7

TENETS OF DISPENSATIONALISM

No description of Dispensationalism can be understood without reference to the three *sine qua non* originally articulated by Charles Ryrie.[124] These three items are the core of Dispensationalism. Trahan recounts these three beliefs:

(1) The recognition of a consistent distinction between Israel and the Church

(2) A consistent and regular use of a literal principle of interpretation

(3) A basic and primary conception of the purpose of God as His own glory rather than the salvation of mankind.

These three points are considered the primary factors that distinguish a *Dispensationalist* from a

---

124 Ryrie, 91.

nondispensationalist. The term *sine qua non* indicates that they are the basic and **indispensable essentials** of Dispensationalism.[125]

A critique of these in light of Covenant Theology is difficult when it comes to the first two essentials. With the second, among evangelical scholarship a consensus cannot be found for when to understand the Bible literally and when to take it figuratively and to what extent. Furthermore, those that hold to Replacement Theology do not recognize precise distinctions between Israel and the Church. Point three is not as significant because speculation about the primary purpose of God is irrelevant to the present discussion. In the same manner that Covenant Theology holds to derived tenets and not explicit teaching, so Dispensationalism does when it comes to speculating on God's primary purpose in the Bible. Even if salvation is the main thrust, as Covenant Theology would presume, could not this salvation point to a higher purpose; that of God's glory? The answer is certainly maybe.

Paul S. Karleen addresses this issue concerning God's ultimate goal in a way that complements the goal stated by Covenant Theology:

> It is worthwhile to ask if there is some overall thing that God is doing in eternity in relation to the universe and the beings that He has made, both human and angelic. We might, for example, suggest that the bottom line is to provide salvation. Although that is certainly important, it is too one-sided and is simply centered on what we get. If that were all, then God would be just a great benefactor, giving us what we need or want.[126]

---

125 Trahan, 65.
126 Karleen.

The goal of Covenant Theology was stated earlier as a way of explaining God's activity in salvation during different periods of time and that God has always had but one way to save mankind, by grace through faith. The goal of Dispensationalism then does not contradict this. Dispensationalism attempts to allow Scripture to be consistent with itself, to explain the obvious differences in how God dealt with man over the course of biblical history. This does not take away from the soteriological methodology used by God, but helps interpret Scripture in light of whatever dispensation the reader may find himself. Dispensationalism is truly an approach to understanding the Bible rather than a system of theology. True enough, Dispensationalism includes certain truths regarding the Church, prophecy, and Israel, but it is basically an outlook on the Bible that works on the basis of historic, orthodox tenets of the faith, and attempts to allow the Bible to open itself to the reader. This is clearly the factor that divides it from other conservative systems of interpretation.[127]

The line between Israel and the Church may be the biggest obstacle blocking harmony between Covenant Theology and Dispensationalism. This underlies the differences between the allegorical method and the literal method. In order to arrive at a belief that the Church is the same as Israel, the plain, literal reading of the text must be ignored or reinterpreted. The idea that the Church is a mystery not spoken of in the Old Testament will be examined in a later chapter.

According to Scofield, each dispensation has certain markers that delineate one dispensation from another and therefore have an objective element that allows for scrutiny:

---

127 Ibid.

The Scriptures divide time (by which is meant the entire period from the creation of Adam to the 'new heaven and a new earth' of Rev. 21:1) into seven unequal periods, usually called dispensations (Eph. 3:2), . . .

These periods are marked off in Scripture by some change in God's method of dealing with mankind, or a portion of mankind, in respect of the two questions: of sin, and of man's responsibility. Each of the dispensations may be regarded as a new test of the natural man, and each ends in judgment, marking his utter failure in every dispensation. Five of these dispensations, or periods of time, have been fulfilled; we are living in the sixth, probably toward its close, and have before us the seventh, and the last: the Millennium.[128]

When the dispensations are examined in the following chapter, this scheme of testing, failure, and judgment will be the basis for evaluation and commentary.

The next chapter will examine the various dispensations found in Scripture. The reason that these are not included in the same chapter including the tenets, as was the case with Covenant Theology, is threefold: (1) the actual number of dispensations is not as important to Dispensationalism as understanding what the reasoning is behind dividing the word of God into dispensations, (2) the tenets of Dispensationalism are interwoven with the time frames in which each take place, (3) there are significantly more dispensations in Dispensationalism than there are covenants

---

128 C.I. Scofield, *Rightly Dividing the Word of Truth* chapter 2 available online http://www.biblebelievers.com/scofield/scofield_rightly02.html (accessed 12/30/2009).

CHAPTER 8

THE BIBLICAL DISPENSATIONS EXAMINED

Before exposition and analysis can be made upon the dispensations that are argued as present in the Bible, the first question that must be answered is just how many dispensations are in the Bible? The answer to this question will depend on who you ask.

Clarence Mason appears to argue for five dispensations, but seems to find the exact number as a matter of unimportance:

> This writer submits that the dispensational viewpoint is inherent in the facts of the Bible's sequence of events. The line of reasoning goes like this: If the fall of man be accepted as a Biblical fact, all Bible believers of whatever theological bracket recognize that there was an essential difference between the state of man before and after that horrendous

event. Again, the Epistle to the Hebrews and other portions of the New Testament labor the distinction between the condition of things before the cross and what obtained after the cross. Some insist upon a more severe transition than others, but the old and the new are not to be confused without disastrous interpretational results. Further, all chiliasts believe another tremendous transitions will take place at the return of the Lord Jesus Christ.

It will be seen, therefore, that we have here at least five different periods with their distinctiveness: (1) Man in a period prior to the fall; (2) man as fallen; (3) man under the Old Covenant, i.e., precross; (4) man since the historic fact of Christ's cross and resurrection; (5) redeemed man as ruling with Christ over a changed earth. It is relatively unimportant if one comes up with exactly seven.[129]

We see here the important distinction that Dispensationalists make between the issues of how God relates to man at different points in the Bible over against the matter of lesser importance to Dispensationalists; that being the number of such changes marking off one dispensation from another. Lewis Sperry Chafer says, "If one does not bring a lamb to the altar in worshipping God, then he is a Dispensationalist. One who worships on Sunday instead of Saturday is also a Dispensationalist, because he recognizes the Sabbath was for Israel, not the Church (Exodus 20:8-11)."[130]

---

129 Clarence E. Mason, Jr., "A Review of Dispensationalism by John Wick Bowman: Part I," *Bibliotheca Sacra.* (Dallas, TX: Dallas Theological Seminary, 1996, c1955-1995). As cited by Trahan, 24.

130 As cited in Trahan, 24.

The quote by Chafer is included to show two things. For one, Chafer is correct that dispensations are clearly taught in and are indispensable to the Bible, but also that one must be careful to judge the motives for behavior. Here Chafer would have anyone who chooses to worship on Saturday as someone who does not understand the difference between the Church and Israel. Because the original apostles worshipped on Sunday, the practice has continued. But there is no hard and fast rule about which day a group can worship – instead this decision is a matter of preference. The early church gathered on Sundays, and the practice has taken root, but nothing prevents a church from having a worship service on Saturday nights. To know the motivations behind why a person does or does not do something that he or she is free to do or not do in Christ is impossible to adduce with certainty. One must be careful when making sharp contrasts between Israel and the Church because the believer may in fact be exercising their freedom in the Age of Grace to follow an Israelite example for their own reasons.

Charles Ryrie likewise finds the names and numbers of dispensations relatively unimportant.[131] Augustus Strong breaks Dispensationalism into two, with the bifurcation being the Old and New Testaments. He sees two dispensations covering history. This is revealed in passing during some helpful comments on Christian living:

> We discern a striking parallel between the predictions of Christ's first, and the predictions of his second, advent. In both cases the event was more distant and more grand than those imagined to whom the prophecies first came. Under both dispensations, patient waiting for Christ was intended to discipline the faith, and to enlarge the conceptions, of God's

---

131 Ryrie, 51.

true servants. The fact that every age since Christ ascended has had its Chiliasts and Second Adventists should turn our thoughts away from curious and fruitless prying into the time of Christ's coming, and set us at immediate and constant endeavor to be ready, at whatsoever hour he may appear.[132]

A Postmillennialist, Strong would be far removed from a modern day Dispensationalist, but it is important to note that even on the most extreme opposite end of pretribulational Premillennialism, a Reformed theologian sees dispensations in the Bible.

An example of a larger number of dispensations is Harold Wilmington. He sees nine dispensations covering the biblical timeline:

> The school of Bible interpretation known as Dispensationalism views the world as a household run by God. God "dispenses," or administers, the affairs of his "household world" in various stages of revelation (see exposition on Eph. 1:7–12).

The Dispensation of Innocence
From Creation to the Fall (Gen. 1:28–3:6)

The Dispensation of Conscience
From the Fall to the Flood (Gen. 4:1–8:14)

The Dispensation of Civil Government
From the Flood to the dispersion at Babel (Gen. 8:15–11:9)

---

132 A.H. Strong, *Systematic Theology* (Bellingham, WA: Logos Research Systems, Inc., 2004), 1007.

The Dispensation of Promise (Patriarchal Rule)
From Babel to Mount Sinai (Gen. 11:10—Exodus. 18:27)

The Dispensation of Mosaic Law
From Mount Sinai to the upper room (Exodus. 19—Acts 1)

The Dispensation of the Bride of the Lamb (the Church)
From the upper room to the Rapture (Acts 2—Rev. 3)

The Dispensation of the Wrath of the Lamb (the Tribulation)
From the Rapture to the Second Coming (Rev. 6:1–20:3)

The Dispensation of the Rule of the Lamb (the Millennium)
From the Second Coming through the Great White Throne Judgment (Rev. 20:4–15)

The Dispensation of the New Creation of the Lamb (the World Without End)
From the Great White Throne Judgment throughout all eternity (Rev. 21–22)[133]

Whether or not the Eternal State is a dispensation, as Wilmington suggests here, is not a dividing point among Dispensationalists, although most would disagree with Wilmington, suggesting that the Millennium is the final dispensation.

---

133 Harold Willmington, *Wilmington's Bible Handbook* (Wheaton, IL: Tyndale House Publishers, 1997), 821.

A key component of Dispensationalism mentioned earlier is the constant circular activity of God's tasking man with responsibility, man failing in an effort to maintain the aspects of the responsibility, judgment from God, and then the beginning of a new cycle. Depending on the number of dispensations one believes are present in the Bible, the same number of cycles mentioned above will be present. As evidenced by just a brief sampling of Dispensationalists, the unity in understanding the meaning of what a dispensation is outweighs the lack of unity concerning the exact number of dispensations. J. B. Tidwell sums up this idea best: "A dispensation is a period of time during which God deals in a particular way with man in the matter of sin and responsibility. The whole Bible may be divided into either three or seven dispensations."[134] Therefore, for what is basically an arbitrary reason, and the fact that seven is a number of biblical significance, this review of the dispensations will break Dispensationalism into what seems to be common number, that of the seven dispensational scheme. Scofield's scheme as found in *Rightly Dividing the Word of Truth* will be used. As mentioned earlier, the form will be the test, failure, and judgment of man in each economy or dispensation. The material for these cycles is from Scofield, but the commentary and evaluation are the author's and are not representative of all Dispensationalists. As to why God would test mankind in such a way, Ryrie explains that, "such tests are not for the purpose of enlightening God but for the purpose of bringing out what is in people, whether faith or failure."[135] As will be seen, when God tasks man with any obligation, as Adam demonstrates, and he in a better position than anyone else who has come after because of his

---

134 J.B. Tidwell, *The Bible Book by Book: A Manual for the Outline Study of the Bible by Books* (Waco, TX: Baylor University Press, 1916).

135 Ryrie, 34.

ability not to sin, the result is always failure to live to the standard God has set. Each failure points more and more to the need of a solution that lies outside of man's ability to be responsible for that which God has entrusted him with.

A. Innocence (Genesis 1:26-3:24)

The Age of Innocence is universally accepted by Dispensationalists to be the first dispensation, though as Ryrie points out in critiquing Progressive Dispensationalism, the agreement extends only to the beginning of this economy. The reason it begins at Genesis 1:26 is due to the fact that a dispensation involves God's interaction with man, and man was not created until Genesis 1:26. Therefore this dispensation involves God and the first couple, Adam and Eve. What is unique about this dispensation is that man was as yet unfallen, and possessed the ability not to sin. The test given by God was to abstain from eating the fruit of the tree of the knowledge of good and evil. The failure of Adam and Eve was total. Given but one command they violated it by any objective measurement. The judgment of God in this dispensation was dismissal from the Garden of Eden. Edmund Clowney, in a less scholarly, but engrossing way, describes Adam's predicament as the first man in the Age of Innocence:

> Adam's freedom would seem to have only one restraint. God pointed out to him one tree in the garden of which he must not eat. A smaller limitation would be hard to imagine. All the fruits of Eden were his to enjoy. All the trees were his to cultivate, all the animals his to call and command. Yet Adam, the son of God, was being tested in his obedience to his Father and Creator. He, the first man, held the destiny of all his descendants, for his

> was the pivotal role. He was the father of those to be born in his image; he represented the race of those who would come from him. By obedience under testing, his righteousness would pass beyond its original innocence. He would know the difference between good and evil by choosing the good. He would be confirmed as the righteous son of God, free to eat of the tree of life forever.[136]

During this first testing of man God is clear and unambiguous in the responsibilities that He gives to man. So clear is the fact that the blessings of God, including eternal life, are based on man keeping the Covenant of Works, that Covenant Theology is forced to admit the different salvific institution found here and adjusts its theology to account for this. Instead of forcing the continuity that has been demonstrated to flow from one dispensation to the next, the complete lack of such evidence compels Covenant Theology to break from the Covenant of Grace, which would be one long unbroken strand of the Covenant of Redemption, if not for the dispensation of innocence. So invasive is this to a Covenant Theology mindset, that a separate covenant, only in effect for less than three chapters, must be created to accommodate this outlying data to their system. But as described earlier, the time period for the Covenant of Works exactly overlaps the Age of Innocence. The different paths the theological camps take diverge from this point, at Genesis 4:1. Because the goal of Dispensationalism is not soteriological in scope, the divergence that has caused disruption in theology for centuries might have been avoided.

---

136 Clowney, 21.

B. Conscience (Genesis 4:1-7:24)

The period of time from the Garden of Eden to the flood is commonly called by Dispensationalists the Age of Conscience. Similar to the time of the Judges, everyone was to do right by the law of their consciences. The individual conscience was the guide or law under which mankind lived. The absence of further covenant promises predominates this period of mankind. No particular assignments other than obedience to God was required during this dispensation. Each person was guided by their own idea of right and wrong. Because of the fall, the propensity for human evil became manifest. The idea of using good moral judgment could be construed as the test during this time although this is nowhere explicitly stated. This dispensation lasted about fifteen hundred years. The failure of mankind during this dispensation was great, to the extent that God is grieved (Genesis 6:6). The judgment during this temptation is perhaps the clearest point drawn out from this dispensation. The Nephilim and the standards of what is right behavior and wrong behavior are anything but clear to the modern day reader. The judgment of the flood, however, is known by Christians and non-Christians alike. The flood destroyed all living things except for Noah, his family, and the animals on the ark.

C. Human Government (Genesis 8:1-11:26)

At the conclusion of the Age of Conscience, the term covenant is introduced as God commits Himself to never again destroy every living thing, even though mankind will demonstrate that it will continue in evil (Genesis 8:21).

The test that God gave man during the Dispensation of Human Government is proper respect for God through national governments over the new, purged world. God established the basis for human civil government by his institution of capital punishment (Genesis 9:6). Under human government, the failure of man is typified by the building of the tower of Babel. The people of this time forsook God's reign for the reign of leaders such as Nimrod. While God would have the peoples of the earth united under God's rule, they instead sought a name and unity for themselves. The tower of Babel, doubtless for the worship of the heavenly bodies, the sun, moon, and stars, became the symbol of mankind's rebellion and failure of the testing that was administered during this stewardship. The judgment by God was the confusion of languages and the scattering of the people abroad on the face of the earth.

It is during this time that Dispensationalism shows its usefulness in setting lines of demarcation and its deficiencies in showing how these changes in dispensations are not related to such changes in covenantal relationships in Scripture. No covenant appears to bridge the gap from the confusing of languages to the time of Abraham. Dispensationalism here does an excellent job showing mankind's reaction to God's administration during a specific time, but one would be hard-pressed to find the Covenant of Grace as present in the Age of Human Government, thus highlighting three things: 1) the Covenant of Grace is soteriological, 2) dispensations can come and go without covenants and 3) covenants and dispensations serve different purposes. The eternal promise of God to redeem mankind always undergirds covenant promises and the judgments after man's failure remind the reader that man cannot meet God's obligations unaided.

D. Promise (Genesis 11:27-Exodus 18:27)

The test of man during the Age of Promise was to keep the conditions of the Abrahamic covenant. God called

Abram (later Abraham) to leave Ur of the Chaldees and come to Canaan. The Age of Promise, as understood by Dispensationalists, began with the covenant promises made by God to Abraham. Some of the promises given to Abraham included personal greatness, national greatness and inheritance of the Land to Abraham and his descendents, and the promise of blessing to all nations through him. This promise of blessing to all nations is called the gospel in Galatians 3:8-9. And Galatians 3:14-29 makes it clear that this was the promise of forgiveness of sins and spiritual life through Abraham's seed, Christ, that is received by faith, by placing faith in God. The object of this faith, the promise of the seed or a general trust in God to be faithful will be discussed later.

Whether this was a unilateral covenant or a bilateral covenant is a matter of debate. Genesis 15 describes the covenant ceremony by which the Lord confirms His promise that Abraham will possess the Land. The details of the ceremony (15:9-21) can be seen in a bilateral fashion; the party who violated the covenant was bound to become like the slain animals. However, instead of walking between the separated bodies Abraham was sent into a deep sleep and was not an active party in the covenant ceremony. This would seem to indicate that the covenant was unilateral. However, other passages in Genesis make it clear that Abraham still had a part to play in the covenant relationship (Gen. 17:1-4; 18:19; 22:2, 16-18; 26:4-5).[137]

Whether or not this covenant is unilateral or bilateral is of some import, as the idea of testing, failure and judgment falls apart under a unilateral approach. In order for man to fail during a dispensation, there must be conditions under

---

137 Ronald Youngblood, "The Abrahamic Covenant: Conditional or Unconditional?" in Morris Inch & Ronald Youngblood, eds. *The Living and Active Word of God* (Winona Lake, IN: Eisenbrauns, 1983), 31-46.

which he can be judged to have either passed or failed. The admonition in Genesis 17:1 to be blameless before God occurs before the covenant is reiterated. If one takes to the bilateral scheme, the failure to walk blameless is obvious, as Abraham and his descendents failed in this area. If, as this work has demonstrated, the promise of God is unconditional to the extent that God will offer a way for mankind to be saved, this promise is similar to the New Covenant promises of Jeremiah and the promise made in the Garden. Therefore the Law will be shown to be an intercalation in this Age of Promise. The promise is more likely an unconditional promise that Abraham and his descendents are unable to keep, but a promise that one in his line will keep the obligations of the dispensation and therefore succeed where all others have failed. In this sense, this dispensation is more akin to the Covenant of Grace and does not fit the failure pattern. But if one were to argue that the covenant was bilateral, then the judgment for failure to be perfect would be the bondage suffered by the Israelites in Egypt, but this is not tied to the covenant, and should be rejected. Perhaps, as Wenham argues, the judgment is in the form of a premature death (cf. Exodus 4:24-26) if circumcision is not performed.[138] However, walking blameless and practicing circumcision do not appear to be of a similar condition. The more likely scenario is that this does not fit the usual mold of a dispensation, but is an announcement that foreshadows the Age of Grace, the Millennium and finally the Eternal State. Perhaps no other dispensation is tied to soteriology as the Age of Promise, as the promises are more than just literal Land ownership, but deal with eternal life and redemption; though the people living in this age would

---

138 Gordon J. Wenham, "The Book of Leviticus," *The New International Commentary on the Old Testament* (Grand Rapids: Eerdmans, 1979), 285-286.

not have grasped such a dense meaning. The sending of Joseph and later his family do not appear to be linked to the covenant that ushered in the dispensation. Therefore it is at this point where a definitive rule concerning dispensational schemes does not fit nicely. In one sense this dispensation is interrupted by the Law, which was as unforeseen as the Church, and picked up again in the Age of Grace, but due to the chronological structure imposed for the purposes of this work, albeit somewhat arbitrarily, the Age of Grace will be treated separately from the Age of Promise.

E. Law (Exodus 19:1-Acts 1:26)

Hodge's third dispensation, commonly the fifth in most dispensational schemes, covers the time from Moses to the coming of Christ. He states,

"The third dispensation of this covenant was from Moses to Christ. All that belonged to the previous periods was taken up and included in this. A multitude of new ordinances of polity, worship, and religion were enjoined. A priesthood and a complicated system of sacrifices were introduced. The promises were rendered more definite, setting forth more clearly by the instructions of the prophets the person and work of the coming Redeemer as the prophet, priest, and king of his people. The nature of the redemption He was to effect and the nature of the kingdom He was to establish were thus more and more clearly revealed. We have the direct authority of the New Testament for believing that the Covenant of Grace, or plan of salvation, thus underlay the whole of the institutions of the Mosaic period, and that their principal design was to teach through types and symbols what is now taught in explicit terms in the gospel. Moses, we are told (Heb. iii. 5), was faithful as a servant to testify concerning the things which were to be spoken after. [139]

The testing that occurred during this dispensation, though not surprisingly omitted by Hodge, a covenantalist with replacement tendencies, was to obey the Mosaic Law out of a love for God. What is often confused by nondispensationalists concerning salvation is explained well by a covenantalist who understands that the Mosaic Law, hereafter referred to as Law, was an important part of God's overall plan of redemption, giving opportunity for faithful Israelites to honor God by obeying the Law, but not as a way of saving even a single soul. This was clearly a dispensation. The Old Testament or Covenant refers specifically to this time period, from the giving of the Law until Christ. This was how God's chosen people were to live in the Land that the Lord their God had given to them.

The Law did provide blessings and curses, and as a bilateral covenant, when the Israelites violated the commandments, both in the wilderness and in the Land, they were driven out, first by the Assyrians, and then by the Babylonians.

There is some disagreement among Dispensationalists as to whether or not this dispensation will resume after the Rapture of the Church. Berl Chisum is representative of this view:

> The Law dispensation was not an uninterrupted age as such. It began with the giving of the Ten Commandments and continued in practice until after the Age of Grace began. It was interrupted by the Age of Grace and it will continue for a space of time after the Age of Grace is over. *It is inseparably*

---

139 Hodge, *Systematic theology*. Originally published 1872, 2:370-377.

> *connected to Israel and God's dealings with them as*
> *a nation.*[140]

This idea could be misleading and has led to the accusation that Dispensationalists believe a return to the Mosaic Law will be part of the Millennium. This is of course contradictory to the idea of progressive revelation and would be invalid if that is what is taught. Dispensationalists who believe a return to the period of Law will occur after the Dispensation of Grace do not believe there will be a return to the Law in the same manner as it was implemented at Sinai. To avoid such confusion, the dispensation of the Millennium, while Jewish in character, is a separate dispensation from the Law. But the overlap is noted and, as with the Age of Promise, certain aspects of dispensations carry over into subsequent dispensations. This work seeks to demonstrate that the Age of Law is more of a parenthesis in the Age of Promise which is resumed in the Age of Grace than the Age of Grace is a parenthesis in the age of Law. To this idea, Dispensationalists may or may not agree.

F. Grace (Acts 2:1-Revelation 19:21)

The test during the Dispensation of Grace is to believe upon the Lord Jesus Christ. This period is new in regards to the Old Covenant of the Law. The New Testament is broadly known as the New Covenant and covers the entirety of the Age of Grace. One of the primary distinctives is the global scope of the New Covenant. The covenant, and therefore the dispensational expectations of this economy are not confined to national Israel, but are available for admittance of all who will believe, no matter what nationality or class of

---

140 Berl Chisum, "Rightly Dividing the Word" http://www.Bibletruths.org/study/rightly.html (accessed 12/14/2009).

man or woman.[141] Perhaps the most radical transformation from one dispensation to the next occurs during the transition from the period of the Law to the Age of Grace. The Church is present in this age and no other before it, and Christ's establishment of such an institution that has Jews and Gentiles worshipping God together without the Law was a mystery revealed during this age. Bruce writes of this aspect:

> In the Pauline writings one aspect of the gospel - the manner and purpose of its communication to the Gentile world – is treated as a 'mystery . . . which was not made known to the sons of men in other generations as it has now been revealed to Christ's holy apostles and prophets in the Spirit' (Ephesians 3:4f.). That the Gentiles would place their hope on the Son of David and rejoice in the God of Israel was affirmed in the Old Testament, as Paul emphasizes in a series of quotations in Romans 15:9-12, but how this prospect would be realized and what its implications would be could not be appreciated until the Gentile mission was launched in the apostolic age.[142]

The failure during this dispensation is unbelief and apostasy, with the judgment of the great tribulation as the signal for the next dispensation. This period of great tribulation concludes the Age of Grace. It is not typically considered a dispensation in and of itself, but as the end of the Age of Grace. The tribulation period, and thus the Age

---

141 Hodge, *Systematic theology*. Originally published 1872, 2:370-377.

142 F. F. Bruce, *The Canon of Scripture* (Downers Grove, IL: InterVarsity Press, 1988, 59.

of Grace, will conclude when Christ returns to earth to establish His Millennial Kingdom.

G. Millennium (Revelation 20:1-22:21)

After Christ returns and establishes His Millennial Kingdom, testing will continue over mankind. This is why the Millennium is seen as a distinct dispensation. This will be the final time whereby men will be tested and given a final opportunity to receive salvation. Lasting one thousand years, Israel will be the greatest nation and universal peace and prosperity will prevail, with even ravenous beasts perfectly tame (Revelation 20:1-6; Isaiah 11:1-16).[143] Chisum writes of some of the characteristics of this age:

> The characteristics of the preceding ages will be in manifestation:
>
> 1. The resurrected saints will be there in innocence to reign with Christ;
> 2. Consciences will have been cleansed and the knowledge of the Lord will cover the earth;
> 3. A man will reign on David's throne in Jerusalem - the perfectly just, all-knowing, all-powerful God-man, the Lord Jesus Christ;
> 4. The previously unrealized promises made to Abraham, Isaac and Jacob will begin to be fulfilled and will continue to be fulfilled forever;
> 5. The Law will be implanted in the hearts of the saved remnant of Israel; and
> 1. God's saving grace will still be extended to children born on earth during that time.[144]

---

143 Chisum.
144 Ibid.

Following the final rebellion and the final destruction of Satan, "all the unrighteous dead of every age will be resurrected to stand before the great white throne on which God sits in judgment. They will be judged according to their works and it will be shown that their names are not written in the book of life because they rejected Christ and His substitutionary death and sufferings for them, and they too will then be cast into the lake of fire."[145]

The Eternal State is described in Revelation 21 and 22. This is not commonly thought of as another dispensation, because God does not place man under any more tests, and man is now glorified and will reign with Christ for eternity.

While each dispensation was examined, an overall comment on the whole idea of the cyclical nature of the dispensations needs to be made. Though there are problems trying to force continuity into the system, and the test, failure, judgment model does not work the same or exactly as Scofield would have the reader believe it works when compared to Scripture, the overall understanding of God stepping into His creation and progressively revealing Himself as well as making promises and placing man under obligations that are sometimes shifting (such as before the flood and after the flood regarding the eating of meat) is sound and biblical.

John Feinberg is perhaps too harsh in his critique, but it is worth mentioning as he does note the lack of full explanation that Dispensationalists sometimes provide when discussing their system:

> Dispensationalists often claim that each dispensation involves a test for man, a failure, and a judgment. While many claim this is a secondary characteristic

---

145 Ibid.

of a dispensation, many take this idea to suggest that what God is doing with history is attempting to demonstrate that man is a failure under all circumstances and thus needs God. . . .

. . . if this is what God is doing with history, it is surely odd. Why does God have to prove anything to anyone? If God says no one is righteous and that none seeks on his own to do God's will (and God surely says that), isn't that enough proof? Is God suspect as a potential liar until he runs history through all the dispensations to prove that he was right all along? Moreover, if God is trying to prove this, why seven times over? Wouldn't two or three times do? Or maybe before we can agree, God needs to prove this in all *possible* economies, and that would surely be more than seven. If this sounds strange, and it does, it suggests that such thinking is utterly wrong-headed.[146]

The error Feinberg makes is that he asks Dispensationalists to prove why God should act in such a way. The obvious rebuttal is to ask, "Why should God not act in such a way?" Surely, if God chose to test man seven times or one hundred times, he has the right. He also assumes God is out to prove that mankind is a failure and finds new ways in which to do this. The wrong-headed thinking is that God is focused on ways in which He can test mankind and show their failure. This misses the point completely. In the midst of testing man, or giving stipulations by which to live, God is also dispensing and revealing His overall plan of grace that He will bestow on these same sinners should they

---

146 Feinberg, 70.

repent. The focus should be on God's grace and not on the failure of man. Therefore the whole idea of man living under different economies is not odd, nor is it a wrong-headed way of thinking, but when properly understood, it is the method by which God continues to show man's failure and for his need of a savior, and the ever-increasing revelation of that savior in the person of Jesus Christ.

As a concept, the idea of testing, failure, and judgment of mankind during dispensations is not incorrect, but neither is it complete. A complete picture, one which focuses on the eternal promise of God, helps the reader to understand that these cycles continue and will continue until Christ returns, and should help to enhance an understanding of what motivates God: His compassion and grace.

Jesus Christ is the only one who has successfully passed a test, met the requirement, and fulfilled the obligations set upon Him. And this is where Feinberg misses the mark as well. Covenant Theology buttresses well with this idea of testing, because in the Covenant of Grace, mankind now has an out, a way of hope. The eternal promise of God to redeem mankind from their sin crosses all boundaries of covenants and dispensations, and a fuller understanding than just Covenant Theology or just Dispensationalism is required to understand God's purposes regarding testing, failure, judgment, and to add to this, redemption and forgiveness. It is this idea, Covenantal Dispensationalism, to which this work brings the two hermeneutical schools together.

PART III.
COVENANTAL
DISPENSATIONALISM

> differ as to the parties, as to the promises, and as to the conditions.[147]

Hodge is on point by skipping over the entire Covenant of Works, not because it is not a reality taught in Scripture, but because of the confusion that arises when considering multiple dispensations, theological covenants, biblical covenants, and even the Old and New Testaments (or covenants). The most important of all covenants in Hodge's mind, as in the author's, is the Covenant of Redemption. The only adjustment to Hodge's otherwise excellent assessment is that the one covenant, which he rightly points out is the eternal covenant made between the Father and the Son, spans not only all dispensations, but also the two covenants, that of grace and works. Though this work has indicted the term covenant in Covenant Theology, if there is one unifying factor, Hodge has hit it on the button. The plan of redemption is part and parcel with the story of the Bible. One would argue that the two covenants, grace and redemption are "clearly revealed" in Scripture, but the principles of God's ultimate plan in saving humanity are revealed throughout the pages of Scripture.

This author would argue that there is only one truly overriding covenant in the mind of God that He has implemented, and it is in affect at all times, but is unveiled in various stages if one were to use the language of "divine" or "theological" covenants. Though sometimes only hinted at (Genesis 3:15), at other times it is made explicitly clear such as in Hebrews 8 and 9. The New Covenant is only new in the sense that the Law is considered the Old Covenant. The Covenant of Redemption is as old as time itself. Prior to the Law, the revealing to humankind of this covenant

---

147 Hodge, *Systematic theology*. Originally published 1872, 2:358-359.

was barely in its infancy stages as far as the full picture of the Covenant of Redemption goes, but there were hints at this covenant nonetheless. Goldsworthy helps explain this idea of redemption:

> This commitment [God's refusal to allow sin to destroy his purpose to make for himself a people in perfect relationship with himself] existed before the rebellion of Adam and Eve, and its expression as a Covenant of Redemption shows that God is ever faithful to his undertakings, even when they are directed toward a people that refuse this love.[148]

The clearest unveiling of the eternal covenant is the promises made to Abram in Genesis 12:13. Wilmington says of these:

> In about the year 2090 B.C., God called Abram to leave the comforts of his homeland and take his family to "the land that I will show you." Abram's speedy response to God's command was the first of several actions on his part that would earn him the title of "spiritual father of those who have faith" (Rom. 4:11, 16).

God made several promises to Abram—promises of seed, soil, and a Savior:

- Abram was to father a great nation *(seed);*
- God would prepare a land for that nation *(soil);*
- the entire world would be blessed by a *Savior* who would come through Abram's seed (Matt. 1:1; Gal. 3:8).

---

148 Goldsworthy, 117.

> While all of Abraham's descendants—the nation of Israel—were commissioned to be a blessing to the world, because of their repeated failure to do so the promise would be fulfilled through Christ (Isaiah 41:1–20; 43:8–13).[149]

Was Abraham the first person "saved" in the Bible. Absolutely not, for Enoch was clearly redeemed, as was Noah and others. Therefore the promise of eternal life began before the promises to Abraham. Chapter 4 surveyed the major covenants of the Bible, but the point of mentioning God's promises here is that these promises, affirmed many more times to Abraham, form the basis to which subsequent promises and covenants refer back to. The Age of Promise is referred to again and again in the New Testament, while previous announcements by God are either not mentioned or vaguely hinted at. This is why the idea of the promise of redemption is connected in such a way to Abraham, and subsequently to Israel. This does not mean that people were not saved before Abraham, but the clearest revelation of the promise of redemption was given to Abraham first.

An interruption then takes place in Exodus 19. This interruption or intercalation is known as the Law. The Law takes on different meanings. Sometimes it refers to the complete Old Testament, sometimes to just the first five books, but to a Dispensationalist, and for the current purposes, it means the Law given at Sinai that was made between God and national Israel. Upon the incarnation of Christ, the New Testament story begins to be told, and it is here where the Law's purpose has been served, and the rules and regulations are no longer necessary as a foreshadowing for what is to come, for the very reason that what the Law

---

149 Wilmington, 14.

pointed to, Jesus Christ, has come in the flesh. In Christian circles the New Testament is often associated with the New Covenant.

A significant parenthesis existed during the time of the Dispensation of the Law, but it is a parenthesis nonetheless. Therefore the New Testament is truly the continuation of the eternal promise of God that began before Genesis 1, and God revealed progressively to mankind. With this understanding, terms such as New and Old can be misleading, as if the New Covenant were not in place until Christ, when in fact, it was not active until Christ, but had been mentioned and foreshadowed all along throughout history and at various times during the Dispensation of the Law.

Clowney, who emphasizes the unfolding plan of Christ as the chief purpose of the Bible, says:

> God's creation is *by* His Son and *for* His Son; in the same way His plan of salvation begins and ends in Christ. Even before Adam and Eve were sent out of Eden, God announced His purpose. He would send His Son into the world to bring salvation (Gen 3:15).[150]

Clowney rightly emphasizes that this plan slowly began to unfold over time. It was not accomplished all at once. God did not "send Christ to be born of Eve by the gates of Eden, nor did He inscribe the whole Bible on the tablets of stone given to Moses at Sinai."[151] Instead, God chose to reveal His plan to save humanity gradually, at various times and packaged in different ways, finally revealed in the person of Christ.

---

150 Edmund P. Clowney, *The Unfolding Mystery: Discovering Christ in the Old Testament* (Phillipsburgh, NJ: Presbyterian and Reformed, 1988), 12.

151 Ibid.

The promise to Abraham is made that from him all nations will be blessed. To David a promise is made that one of his descendents shall sit on the throne forever. To Jeremiah a New Covenant is promised, and finally, in the fullness of time, God sent forth His only son as the Messiah, the fullness of the promise, the evidence that God is faithful, and with this shift several things happened at once that were previously a mystery. The law is abrogated, Israel is no longer the "only" chosen people of God, in fact it is revealed that only to the extent that Israel believed in God were even Israelites chosen before the time of Christ, the Church of Jesus Christ is established, and the Covenant of Redemption shines forth to envelop everyone who will call on the name of the Lord with saving power. This is the fulfillment of the promise. It transcends and reshapes dispensations that came: the crooked road of Eden, the flood, Babel, the years in Egypt, the Exodus, the Law, the Exile are all now understood as pathways on the road of promise to redeem mankind who sinned in Adam and were under a curse. Christ became the curse for mankind, standing in mankind's place to accept the full punishment for sin, and the promise is eternal life for all those who will believe. All dispensations and covenants must reflect this fact if they are to do justice to God's plan of redemption.

While salvation is not necessary the primary purposes of the Bible as Covenant Theology would suggest[152], neither is God's glory the only purpose[153], they are both essential and of utmost importance. The importance of God's actions in restoring mankind from its fallen state by means of Jesus Christ is just as important, but so is the purpose of telling the story of God's chosen people, teaching about the attributes of God, among other things. The Bible is a book where

---

152 So Trahan, 177.
153 Ibid.

Christ calls sinners to Himself and is glorified when one goes from the damnation found by the children of Adam, to a right relationship with God by coming to faith in Christ and placing faith in His completed work on the cross.

It is not as if Covenant Theology and Dispensationalism are engaged in a contest, as they both try to understand God's revelation as best they can, but if they were Dispensationalism would score a point for its explanation of the object of salvation. Clearly, when contemplating the promise of God, one cannot identify the object of belief based on the current situation where one finds himself for to do so would create multiple ways of salvation. Covenant Theology attempts to show that salvation given to Old Testament saints was based upon a "looking forward" towards Christ. John 8:56 is sometimes used to support this. Shedd, for instance states:

> As the doctrine of the Trinity is found in the Old Testament, so is that of the Redeemer. As there is an Old Testament Trinitarianosm, so there is an Old Testament Christology. Both doctrines, however, are less clearly revealed under the former economy than under the latter. Christ is explicit in asserting that the doctrine of his person is found in the Old Testament: "Many prophets and righteous men have desired to see those things which you see" (Matt. 13:17); "Abraham saw my day and was glad" (John 8:56; cf. 12:41; Luke 24:27); "the prophets searched diligently what the Spirit of Christ which was in them did signify, when it testified beforehand

the sufferings of Christ and the glory that should
follow"[154] (1 Pet. 1:10–12).[155]

What is clear by Abraham's looking forward to Christ is
obviously not a looking forward to Jesus' death for sinners;
for even Jesus' own disciples did not fully understand until
Christ rose from the dead. Instead, What Abraham looked
forward to was a faithful God who is faithful to fulfill
His promises. He does so in Jesus Christ. In the same way
in Hebrews 11:10, Abraham doubtfully understood the
heavenly Jerusalem as the location of the redeemed, but
in a sense, by believing in God and trusting him, he was
"looking for the city that has foundations, whose architect
and builder is God."

Covenant Theology can and should be applauded for
its desire to preserve what is truly the only way sin can be
forgiven, but some allowance must be made for those before
the cross without having to render them predictors of the
future.

What is clear is that salvation is in God's mind
throughout His revelation of the covenant of promise. What
Covenant Theology and Dispensational Theology cannot
understand, and the reason for this is lack of evidence, is
exactly what type of faith, or how much faith, one had to
have before the elements of the gospel were fully revealed in
order to be saved.

One may question how the author can be critical
of Covenant Theology and then utterly usurp one of

---

154 Shedd: The patristic and Reformation divines find both the Trinity
and the God-man in the Old Testament. Irenaeus (*Against Heresies* 4.33–34)
makes ample quotations in proof of both doctrines. For the Lutheran and
Reformed citations, see Gerhard, Chemnitz, Hase, Heppe, and Schweitzer
in locis.

155 W. G. T. Shedd and A.W. Gomes, *Dogmatic Theology* (Phillipsburg, NJ: Presbyterian and Reformed, 2003), 612.

the covenants therein to help bridge the gap between Dispensationalism and Covenant Theology. The reason is that the problems with Covenant Theology are not with the theology, but where adherents of Covenant Theology have taken the theology. This is in part due to the use of the term "covenant" for something other than biblical covenantal language, but mostly due to the repeated poor hermeneutics from the Middle Ages onwards. The idea of a Covenant of Redemption is valid even if one chooses not to call it a "covenant." To this idea of a Covenant of Redemption, and only this, does Covenantal Dispensationalism borrow from Covenant Theology. While the Covenant of Works and grace are valid, too, the author believes the term "covenant" has reached its limit of usefulness with the Covenant of Redemption. But again, this is an artificial line in the sand also.

CHAPTER 10

THE LAW AS AN INTERCALATION IN
THE PROGRAM OF PROMISE

One of the problems within the traditional understanding
of Dispensationalism is how the Church is to be understood
and dealt with. In Chapter 12, the establishment of the
difference between the Church and Israel will be explained,
but for now, it suffices to say along with Chafer that:

(1) Any person is a Dispensationalist who trusts
the blood of Christ rather than bringing an animal
sacrifice. (2) Any person is a Dispensationalist who
disclaims any right or title to the land which God
covenanted to Israel for an everlasting inheritance.
And (3) any person is a Dispensationalist who
observes the first day of the week rather than the
seventh. To all this it would be replied that every
Christian does these things, which is obviously true;
and it is equally true that, to a very considerable
degree, all Christians are Dispensationalists.
However, not all Christians, though sincere, are

as well instructed in the spiritual content of the Scriptures as others, nor have they seen the necessity of recognizing other and deeper distinctions which do confront the careful student of the Word of God."[156]

So where does the Church fit in to God's plan for Israel? Dispensationalism would say that the Church is an intercalation in God's overall plan for Israel.[157] The Church is a parenthesis in the plan of God to account for the times of the Gentiles, and will end at the Rapture of the Church.[158] This is tied with the two separate destinies, one for Israel and one for the Church that has long been tied to the teachings of Dispensationalism.

In this chapter, the idea of the Law will be addressed as it fits into the one eternal promise of God to save mankind. Galatians will be the primary text used to explain the Law's role along with common sense. For one example for the realm of common sense, the example of murder will be given. Because the Law has been abrogated, is it therefore condoned behavior to murder another person? Of course it is not. One did not need the law to know that murder is wrong. But the Law and its peculiar intricacies served a vital purpose in God's plan. The main role of the Law is explained by Paul in Galatians 3:10-29. To the mystery of the Church, which was unrevealed until the New Testament and reaches the fulfillment of Christ's plans for the Jews and the Gentiles should be added the mystery of the Law, or at least its temporary nature. For the Jews did not understand Christ's fulfillment of the Law; they believed the Law would

---

156 Lewis S. Chafer, *Dispensationalism* (Dallas: Dallas Seminary Press, 1936), 9.

157 Ryrie.

158 Ibid.

eternally be a set of rules to follow, and even without a Temple they tried to keep the food laws, circumcision and Sabbaths. The Church is a mystery that Paul uses much space in his writings to explain, but the Law's purpose was also a mystery, for the true waiting for promise fulfillment was not from Pentecost to the Rapture, but from Sinai to Bethlehem.

The Law and how it relates to salvation has been a point of contention between the two systems. How does one identify a saved person? Just how would one know who is or who is not elect? The answer to this question is important in understanding the temporary nature of the Law. An unfortunate part of dialogue between the hermeneutical schools is one where Dispensationalists are accused of saying that Israel was saved in some fashion by doing the works of the Law. The turning point in salvation history is obviously the death, burial and resurrection of Jesus Christ. He established His Church, and now everyone who believes in Christ as the risen son of God has eternal life. This standard establishes what one must truly believe in order to be saved. There have always been certain people who have professed these things to be true, but without believing these truths in their heart. The issue is whether that is authentic faith or just a declaration of possessing faith. While one can never know if someone else has made a true commitment to the Christian faith, at least the criteria for salvation is well understood and established. The problem is how to determine what that criteria is in an era before Christ. Each side of the argument has an explanation, but both are deficient.

Covenant Theology would grapple with Hebrews 11 to show that since the time of Abraham, salvation rested on how one looked forward to the anticipation of Christ and His sacrifice. This is a slippery slope as well because to what degree would one have to look forward and how much of the coming crucifixion could they see? How much would they have to understand and accept in order to be a member of the Church, an institution not yet in existence?

The charge against Dispensationalists is that they see salvation as how one looks at the revelation of God as presently bestowed when judging whether a person is saved. This leads to the idea of keeping the Law as a means for Old Testament saints to earn salvation; a wholly unorthodox view of salvation even in the eyes of Dispensationalists.

A guaranteed accurate measuring stick in identifying whether a person is elector o not before the full gospel was given is not possible given the complexities of the biblical record. Hebrews 11 demonstrates various ways that believers expressed their faith in God. And that is the key. Clearly Seth didn't hearken back to God's protevangelium in the garden and gain salvation based on a belief that one day an offspring of Eve would defeat Satan. The point the author of Hebrews makes is that faith shows itself in different ways, but always by trust in God.

Salvation within the Old Testament is a problem as well for Dispensationalism. An example of this difficulty is found within the Dallas Theological Seminary doctrine statement (see Introduction). To restate:

> We believe also that they did not understand the redemptive significance of the prophecies or types concerning the sufferings of Christ (1 Pet. 1:10–12); therefore, we believe that their faith toward God was manifested in other ways as is shown by the long record in Hebrews 11:1–40. We believe further that their faith thus manifested was counted unto them for righteousness (cf. Rom. 4:3 with Gen. 15:6; Rom. 4:5–8; Heb. 11:7).[159]

---

159 http://www.dts.edu/about/doctrinalstatement/ (accessed 09/23/2009).

The reason this is problematic is that the faith described in Hebrews 11 is a humanly grounded faith as opposed to a divine bestowal of faith via monergism often found in the Pauline descriptions of regeneration; a process which tends to minimize the role of the sinner in the process of coming to faith. Terry Wilder points this out:

> Faith, then, in Hebrews, is *being faithful*, and faithfulness is demonstrated in the context of testing and adversity. Faith is active, world engaging, and at times world countering. It is quite simply, a commitment to *please God* through what one does (10:38; 11:5,6; 13:21), a commitment that often will entail hostility from the world. The writer's concern for faithfulness on the part of his readers, emphasizing the *human response* rather than divine impartation, stands in notable contrast to the Pauline accent on faith as a divine gift, independent of human activity.[160]

If a litmus test were to be developed and used in determining the line of demarcation between salvation and damnation during the dispensations prior to the first advent of Christ, such a test would be on an individual, case by case basis, and there is no adequate way to define this dogmatically. Therefore Dallas Theological Seminary's statement is an attempt to escape the dilemma, but instead shows that Dispensationalists do not have a better answer than Covenant theologians as to explain salvation in a clearly definable way before Christ.

---

160 Terry L. Wilder, J. Daryl Charles, and Kendell Easley, *Faithful to the End: An Introduction to Hebrews through Revelation* (Nashville, TN: Broadman and Holman Publishing, 2007), 16.

How they crossed the threshold of salvation will always remain a mystery, but by grace through faith in God is a must. Due to the fact that the present day reader of Scripture has the entire biblical record, one can know now that when a person places his or her faith in Christ they are shown to ratify their election in Christ; for the present discussion ignoring false professors, apostates, or any other type of non-salvific expression of faith. The person is elect because at some point they came to faith in Christ. This is cleaner, more transparent, and more of a bright line test now that God has sent forth His Son. To take this same rationale and work backwards to apply the same sort of standard to dispensations of incomplete revelation is a difficult task. One must leave it to God to determine for Himself how a person reached an appropriate amount of faith to be deemed elect before faith in the substitutionary death of Christ was known, but clearly the responsibility of man has always been to have faith in God to the extent He has revealed Himself.

Before leaving Hebrews, there is an important concept that Dispensationalists appear to have a better handle on than Covenantalists, and that is the continuity and discontinuity throughout the Bible. Terry Wilder has a good example of this as related to a theme only tangentially related to the present discussion, that of the Old Testament versus the New Testament:

> Covenant expresses itself in two ways in Hebrews: similarity (continuity) and difference (discontinuity). Similarity is evidenced, for example, in the writer's use of type and antitype between Israel and the Church; both have been the chosen people of God (4:9; 11:25). Difference is demonstrated, for example, in the superiority of the New Covenant that has been mediated by Jesus (implicitly and

explicitly in chapters 1, 8, 9, and 10). The New Covenant is "better" because it is abiding; it lasts forever (5:6; 7:17, 21, 24, 28: 9:12, 14; 13:20). We should keep in mind the standard ratification of any binding covenant to the ancient mind, whether that covenant is human or divine: blood. In Hebrews blood is both purificatory and ratifying.[161]

The New Covenant is the only covenant believers are responsible for in the current Dispensation of Grace. This covenant was ratified and put into affect by Christ, but it was promised beforehand, and foreshadowed in the Old Covenant, with explicit mention in Jeremiah 31, but there was certainly a covenant relationship in place before the Old Covenant regarding salvation. As has been shown, there were covenants before Sinai, and this work has sought to present and defend the argument that one overriding and overarching covenant has been in place since before the Garden of Eden; that of the promise of redemption. This covenant is now entered into by faith in the fully revealed gospel, but its efficacy was available before its ratification by Christ.

While the different biblical covenants, including the two major divisions of the protestant Bible, were discussed in Chapter 4, the principle of discontinuity is established and is germane to the understanding of the Law as an intercalation in the overall plan of promise. Paul's theology is distinct from Hebrews, with a perspective from God's work in salvation as opposed to human response, but he captures the discontinuity of the New Covenant which was signaled by Christ's shed blood and helps the reader understand that discontinuity is really an unveiling and

---

161 Ibid, 24.

revelation of what was only seen dimly from the Law. It is not so much discontinuity that Paul expounds upon, but rather he helps the Galatians understand the purpose of the law, and whereas Hebrews highlights the ratification of the New Covenant by the shed blood of Christ, Paul helps readers to see that the shed blood and other stipulations of the law served a purpose for a time, but are not obsolete. Therefore the same conclusion is reached by the author of Hebrews as that of Paul, though their paths are quite different.

What is the purpose of the Law then, if the Law has been abrogated and is no longer the standard by which men must be held accountable? Hodge says of this:

> The abolition of the Mosaic dispensation indicates no change in God's plan; it is rather the execution of his plan. Christ's coming and work were no sudden makeshift, to remedy unforeseen defects in the Old Testament scheme: Christ came rather in "the fulness of the time" (Gal. 4:4), to fulfill the "counsel" of God (Acts 2:23). Gen. 8:1 - "God remembered Noah" – interposed by special act for Noah's deliverance, showed that he remembered Noah. While we change, God does not. There is no fickleness or inconstancy in him. Where we once found him, there we may find him still, as Jacob did at Bethel (Gen. 35:1, 6, 9). Immutability is a consolation to the faithful, but a terror to God's enemies (Mal. 3:6—"I, Jehovah, change not; therefore ye, O sons of Jacob, are not consumed"; Ps. 7:11—"a God that hath indignation every day"). It is consistent with constant activity in nature and in grace (John 5:17—"My Father worketh even until now, and I work"; Job 23:13, 14—"he is in one mind, and who can turn him? ... For he performeth

that which is appointed for me: and many such things are with him"). If God's immutability were immobility, we could not worship him, any more than the ancient Greeks were able to worship Fate."[162]

A common answer to why the Law was put in place is that it was to reveal sin. The apostle Paul says as much in Romans 7:7-13, stating that without the law he would not be aware of his violation of the Law. But this answer does not cohere precisely with the unfolding promise of God to bring about the restoration of man through a savior. Under this heading, the purpose of law is given in Galatians:

> [15] To give a human example, brothers: even with a man-made covenant, no one annuls it or adds to it once it has been ratified. [16] Now the promises were made to Abraham and to his offspring. It does not say, "And to offsprings," referring to many, but referring to one, "And to your offspring," who is Christ. [17] This is what I mean: the law, which came 430 years afterward, does not annul a covenant previously ratified by God, so as to make the promise void. [18] For if the inheritance comes by the law, it no longer comes by promise; but God gave it to Abraham by a promise.

> [19] Why then the law? It was added because of transgressions, until the offspring should come to whom the promise had been made, and it was put in place through angels by an intermediary. [20] Now an intermediary implies more than one, but God is one.

---

162 A.H. Strong, 258.

²¹ Is the law then contrary to the promises of God? Certainly not! For if a law had been given that could give life, then righteousness would indeed be by the law. ²² But the Scripture imprisoned everything under sin, so that the promise by faith in Jesus Christ might be given to those who believe.

²³ Now before faith came, we were held captive under the law, imprisoned until the coming faith would be revealed. ²⁴ So the, the law was our guardian until Christ came, in order that we might be justified by faith. ²⁵ But now that faith has come, we are no longer under a guardian, ²⁶ for in Christ Jesus you are all sons of God, through faith. ²⁷ For as many of you as were baptized into Christ have put on Christ. ²⁸There is neither Jew nor Greek, there is neither slave nor free, there is no male and female, for you are all one in Christ Jesus. ²⁹ And if you are Christ's, then you are Abraham's offspring, heirs according to promise (Galatians 3:15-29).[163]

Here Paul references the prison, similar to the earlier reason for the Law in that it exposes sin, but he also points to the promise of God. Paul traces the promise not to the Garden, but to Abraham, as the situation in which he found himself during this letter was to combat a return to Jewish Law. But the point of these statements by Paul was to show that the Law was a guardian, or a pedagogue or schoolmaster. Strong explains that a pedagogue was "a tutor i.e. a guardian and guide of boys. Among the Greeks and the Romans the name was applied to trustworthy slaves who were charged with the duty of supervising the life and

---

163 *The Holy Bible : English standard version.* 2001 (Galatians 3:15-29). Wheaton: Standard Bible Society.

morals of boys belonging to the better class. The boys were not allowed so much as to step out of the house without them before arriving at the age of manhood."[164] The Law was not the full revelation of Jesus Christ, but was certainly part of the progression of revelation of the one to whom the promises of God were made. The Law is no longer applicable to Dispensationalists or to Covenantalists, but it served a noble purpose in the overall plan of God. This was a mystery that was previously hidden, but revealed upon Christ's coming. Paul had to correct a group that did not understand that, and today there is now a large group of believers who have misappropriated the term mystery. To this topic, this work now turns.

The mystery as something unnamed as an institution comprised of more than one ethnic group was certainly hidden in the Old Testament, but a group defined by faith in God is consistently found from Adam to Abel to Noah to Abraham to Moses to David and so on. This is but one of many "mysteries" found in the New Testament.

Because Dispensationalists have said the "mystery" Paul refers to is the Church, it is important to take a brief look at the different ways Paul used the word "mystery" in his letters. Kenneth Barker states:

> The so-called mystery religions of Paul's day used the Greek word *mysterion* in the sense of something that was to be revealed only to the initiated. Paul himself, however, used it to refer to something formerly hidden or obscure but now revealed by God for all to know and understand. The word is used of (1) the incarnation (1 Timothy 3:16), (2)

---

164 J. Strong, *The exhaustive concordance of the Bible : Showing every word of the text of the common English version of the canonical books, and every occurrence of each word in regular order.* (electronic ed.) (G3807).(Ontario: Woodside Bible Fellowship), 1996.

the death of Christ (1 Cor 2:7), (3) God's purpose to sum up all things in Christ (Ephesians 1:9) and especially to include both Jews and Gentiles in the NT Church (Ephesians 3:3-6), (4) the change that will take place at the resurrection (1 Cor 15:51), and (5) the plan of God by which both Jew and Gentile, after a period of disobedience by both, will by His mercy be included in His kingdom (Romans 11:25).[165]

The Church, per se, is not a mystery, but the idea that Jews and Gentiles will worship together without the Mosaic Law is a mystery.[166] While this sounds like mere semantics, it is important to note that when Dispensationalists talk of Israel they are not speaking of Israel as a group of "redeemed" people only, but Israel as understood to include believing and unbelieving Jews. The covenant theologian would refer to Israel as only "spiritual" Israel or a redeemed remnant. The "spiritual" Israel terminology is not biblical however, for God only speaks of Israel in national terms. The fact that the Church is made up of only the redeemed and no unbelievers points to a discontinuity between the Church and Israel.

One cannot say however, as Mills does, that the entire Church Age is a mystery. Mills says the Church Age is the mystery period (Ephesians 3:1-12) and not revealed in the Old Testament.[167] But this age is characterized by the New Covenant of Jeremiah 31:31 which was revealed in the Old Testament. Though originally made with Israel and Judah,

---

165 Kenneth Barker, General Editor, *The Zondervan NASB Study Bible* (Grand Rapids, MI: Zondervan, 1999), 1652.

166 See Bruce, *Canon.*

167 M. Mills, *The Life of Christ: A study guide to the Gospel record* (Dallas, TX: 3E Ministries, 1999).

the New Covenant is inaugurated by Christ and includes the Church in the promises of covenant blessing.[168]

---

168 Other references to a mystery include several uses of the term in Daniel and in the HCSB, Jesus refers to the "secret" of the kingdom of God in Mark 4:11, although other translations such as the AV/KJV render *mysterion* here as "mystery."

CHAPTER 11

WHAT ABOUT REPLACEMENT THEOLOGY?

Replacement Theology, also known as supersessionism, has become associated with Covenant Theology. The tie that binds this view to Covenant Theology is how one views the people who are under the Covenant of Grace. The argument would be that the Covenant of Grace covers just one people of God, therefore ruling out a distinction between different "peoples of God." Because there has always been one people of God, the Church is the natural replacement for national Israel or next step in the development of God's redeemed people.

Before discussing the problems found in Replacement Theology, a brief history of and introduction to different types of supersessionism will lay some groundwork.

Punitive supersessionism is the belief that Israel has been superseded by the Church as a form of punishment, or retribution, for their rejection of their messiah. The Jews have been displaced and ejected out of the covenant of God. Gabriel J. Fackre defines this form of supersessionism as one that "holds that the rejection of Christ both eliminates Israel from God's covenant love and provokes divine retribution."[169] This view was common in the early Church. Hippolytus, Origen, and Lactantius are just a few of the many early Church Fathers who believed that this was the proper understanding of why Israel was rejected and expelled from receiving the covenant blessings of God.

Martin Luther also held to this view, which may explain his apparent anti-Semitism found within some of his writings. He explains that the Jews are no longer the chosen people of God:

> "Listen, Jew, are you aware that Jerusalem and your sovereignty, together with your temple and priesthood, have been destroyed for over 1,460 years?"...For such ruthless wrath of God is sufficient evidence that they assuredly have erred and gone astray. . . . Therefore this work of wrath is proof that the Jews, surely rejected by God, are no longer his people, and neither is he any longer their God.[170]

A modern day supersessionist is Graeme Goldsworthy, who completely dismisses the relevance of national Israel in the future fulfillment of God's promises:

> Now Jesus, the true Israel and the new temple, is telling his disciples that the Holy Spirit takes his presence into the entire world through the

---

169 Gabriel J. Fackre, *Ecumenical Faith in Evangelical Perspective* (Grand Rapids: Eerdmans, 1993), 148.

170 Martin Luther, "On the Jews and Their Lies," in "Three Categories of Supersessionism" by Michael J. Vlach, http://www.theologicalstudies.org/page/page/1572335.htm (accessed December 22, 2009).

preaching of the gospel. In this way the nations will be gathered to Christ, who takes the place of the old Israel and Jerusalem...Jesus is actually saying that Jerusalem and the temple have been superseded. The focal point of the kingdom is no longer a building in the land of Judah, rather it is himself, wherever his presence is to be found. After he exchanges his bodily presence for his presence by the Spirit, the Gentiles will be brought to the new temple that is created by that Spirit wherever the gospel is preached.[171]

In this view of supersessionism, Christ is not only the new Israel, but is in fact the Temple as well. This delving into complete allegorizing and spiritualization of the Old Testament is typical of modern day Covenantal theologians.

Vern Poythress has a different take on supersessionism that all Christians are the true Israel:

Because Christ is an Israelite and Christians are in union with Christ, Christians partake of the benefits promised to Israel and Judah in Jeremiah. With whom is the New Covenant made? It is made with Israel and Judah. Hence it is made with Christians by virtue of Christ the Israelite. Thus one might say that Israel and Judah themselves undergo a transformation at the first coming of Christ, because Christ is the final, supremely faithful Israelite. Around him all true Israel gathers.[172]

---

171 Goldsworthy, 212-13.

172 Vern S. Poythress, *Understanding Dispensationalists*, 2nd ed. (Phillipsburg, NJ: Presbyterian & Reformed, 1994), 106.

This was also the view of many throughout the early Christianity. The promise of redemption was a unilateral covenant God made with man. It was not dependent on obedience to the Law. Therefore, despite Israel's disobedience, He accepts those of Israel who believe in the Messiah, and any Gentiles who believe in Israel's Messiah share in the blessings of the covenant. Karl Barth and N.T. Wright are more modern advocates of this view. Barth stated:

> The first Israel, constituted on the basis of physical descent from Abraham, has fulfilled its mission now that the Saviour of the world has sprung from it and its Messiah has appeared. Its members can only accept this fact with gratitude, and in confirmation of their own deepest election and calling attach themselves to the people of this Saviour, their own King, whose members the Gentiles are now called to be as well. Its mission as a natural community has now run its course and cannot be continued or repeated.[173]

N.T. Wright states that "Israel's purpose had come to its head in Jesus' work. Those who now belonged to Jesus claimed to be the continuation of Israel in a new situation."[174] He adds, "Jesus intended those who responded to Him to see themselves as the true, restored Israel."[175]

Zuck explains the biblical rationale for what he sees as a quasi-Replacement Theology in Hebrews:

> Another support for this view is the line of thought advanced in (Hebrews) 7:28. Here the author

---

173 Karl Barth, *Church Dogmatics* III/2, 584.

174 N.T. Wright, *The New Testament and the People of God* (Minneapolis: Fortress, 1992), 457.

175 N.T. Wright, *Jesus and the Victory of God* (Minneapolis: Fortress, 1996), 316.

presented the law and its high priests as a temporary provision to be superseded by God's later provision. The oath of Psalm 110:4 "came after the law" to appoint Jesus as the eternal and perfect High Priest. Just as Paul argued in Galatians 3:15–29 (somewhat differently) that the law was a temporary arrangement designed to lead to Christ, the author of Hebrews pictured the work of God in the Son as the culminating event in salvation-history, marking the fulfillment and abrogation of the law. This event marks the inauguration of the New Covenant, as chapter 8 then states.

The work of God in Christ inaugurates a new era in the fulfillment of God's plan, but some aspects of that plan are yet to be fulfilled.[176]

The theologians surveyed, and many throughout the ages, have wrestled with how to keep continuity between Israel and the Church, and supersessionism was a common effort to do just that. But the fact that promises were made to Israel as a nation and an ethnic group of people cannot be broken or transferred to an entity that did not exist at the time. The Church was established by Jesus and not before. Promises made to a group of people that included redeemed and unredeemed persons would not logically be transferred to only redeemed people.

Enns describes the differences as thus:

---

176 R. B. Zuck, *A Biblical Theology of the New Testament* (Chicago: Moody Press, 1996), 402.

> The term *Israel* always refers to the physical posterity
> of Jacob; nowhere does it refer to the Church.[177]
> Although nondispensationalists frequently refer to
> the Church as the "new Israel," there is no biblical
> warrant for doing so. Many passages indicate Israel
> was still regarded as a distinct entity after the birth
> of the Church (Rom. 9:6; 1 Cor. 10:32). Israel was
> given unconditional promises (covenants) in the
> Old Testament that must be fulfilled with Israel in
> the Millennial Kingdom. The Church, on the other
> hand, is a distinct New Testament entity born at
> Pentecost (1 Cor. 12:13) and not existing in the Old
> Testament, nor prophesied in the Old Testament
> (Eph. 3:9).[178]

When Christ came, there was a radical re-definition
of who the people of God are, and the Church is a more
accurate picture than the one previously given in the Old
Testament. The New Covenant is between God and only
those who have faith in Christ; whereas portions of the Law
and the Old Covenant were to a theocratic society, with its
mixture of believers and the faithless.

The eternal promise of God reached a climactic moment
at the cross, and while aspects of the complete picture of God's
fulfillment of this promise have yet to reach their conclusion
in history, one can be assured that God is faithful to His
promise. Replacement Theology and supersessionism are
poor terms when it comes to understanding the relationship
between the Church and Israel. Barth and Wright come

---

177 The only passage that is somewhat debatable is Galatians 6:16.
The Greek *kai* should probably be understood epexegetically as "even." Israel
of God thus refers to believing Israelites who walk by faith and not as the
legalistic Judaizers.

178 Enns, 389.

close to the most accurate way of understanding Christ in relationship to both. The eternal promise of God to redeem mankind must take a forefront when viewing Israel and the Church. The Law given to Israel certainly foreshadowed much of what was to come in the person of Christ, but God repeatedly referred to the nation Israel as His chosen nation.

The following facts can be gleaned from this survey of the history of supersessionism: Israel is not the Church. The Church did not exist before Pentecost. The Covenant of Grace bestowed upon the elect in Christ was pictured before Christ's incarnation in the people of God, the Israelites, with the Law as a custodian until the fulfillment of the law, Jesus Christ, came to fulfill the law. To the Israelites promises were made that will be fulfilled at a time future to the present. The covenant made with Israel and Judah is extended to all those in the Church, as it is effective only for Israelites who were elect of God in a future Millennial Kingdom upon the return of Christ. The tangible, material promises made by God to give Israel a Land are not transferred somehow to the Church. The two are distinct; one did not replace the other. So with a clear distinction between Israel and the Church, the next chapter deals with the ramifications of these distinctions and how the progressively revealed plan of God applies to Israel and to the Church.

What is interesting about this replacement theory is that its advocates mean well and would like to protect the uniformity of Scripture and the continuity between the testaments, but they misunderstand Dispensationalism. As mentioned earlier, not all of Israel is elect. Only those of faith are covered under the Covenant of Grace in the Old Testament, or the Covenant of Redemption. Because the Church is made up entirely of believers, the destiny is similar for all members. Because Israel is comprised of nonbelievers

Would they be considered Israelites? The answer is of course no. In a spiritual sense they would be part of God's people that stretches from (presumably) Adam to the last person who will ever be saved, but Noahites are no more Israel than Israel is the Church.

Jesus told Peter, "And I also say to you that you are Peter, and on this rock I will build My Church, and the forces of Hades will not overpower it." Whether or not the rock upon which Jesus will build His Church is Peter[179] or Peter's confession that Jesus is the Messiah (verse 16)[180] is inconsequential to the study of whether or not the Church is a separate entity from Israel. The truly important thing to find out is who are the members of the Church and does it include Old Testament saints, tribulation saints, all of the above, or only Gentiles and Jews from Pentecost to the Rapture?

Jesus uses the word *oikoumene* in this instance to describe what Christ will do. Of more importance than the word meaning "to build a house or to found, establish[181]" is the verb tense. Found here it is in the first person, future, active, indicative implying that this is something Jesus will do in the future. Whether this is done at Pentecost or sometime a few years before when Jesus called His disciples is not germane to the present discussion. What is important to note is that the Church is something completely new that did not exist before Christ's establishment of it. A possible rebuttal to this would be that *oikoumene* can also mean "to restore

---

179 So S.T. Bloomfield, *The Greek Testament with English Notes,* Vol. I (Boston: Perkins & Marvin, 1837) as well as D.A. Carson, "Matthew" *The Expositor's Bible Commentary,* Volume 8. Frank Gaebelien, Ed., (Grand Rapids: Zondervan).

180 So W. C. Allen, *A Critical and Exegetical Commentary on the Gospel According to Matthew* (Edinburgh: T&T Clark, 1907).

181 J. Strong, (G3618).

by building, to rebuild, repair."[182] While this definition is certainly a possible one for *oikoumene*, the context of this usage would make the application of this definition unlikely as the remainder of the quotation by Jesus states: "the gates of hell shall not prevail against it (it being the Church)." If Jesus were merely rebuilding an edifice that had fallen into disrepair from what the Church was originally meant to be, and thereby simply using a new term for the old idea of spiritual Israel, it is unlikely that Christ would state that the gates of hell shall not prevail against it, as though had He not done the repairing, the Church might not withstand the gates of hell and be overrun. Clearly this is a qualitatively different program Christ was establishing, and it was to be done in the future (with respect to the time that Jesus said this to Peter after Peter's acknowledgement that Jesus is the Christ, the Son of the living God (Matthew 16:16)).

So if the Church is not the same as Israel or spiritual Israel (defined going forward over against ethnic Israel, spiritual Israel includes not only ethnic believing Jews, but Gentile proselytes, God-fearers and any who might be considered a member of God's family through faith in Christ), how is Israel to be understood in the New Testament?

The promises to Israel stand. God will not go back on His word. However, because of progressive revelation, the promises of God can now be understood to include both Israel and the Church. Saved Israel and the Church will share in the as of yet unfulfilled promises connected to the Abrahamic and New Covenant. Obviously the Land covenant is made with Israel, but the Church will spend eternity in the Land with Christ as well. Just because the Church may not have been prophesied about specifically in the Old Testament (Eph. 3:9),[183] does not mean the

---

182 Ibid.
183 Enns, 389.

promises to Israel do not apply to the Church. Again, one cannot skip over the Church Age and pick up with the Law in the Millennial Kingdom. Christ was the goal of the Law, and expansion, not parenthesis, should be normative when thinking of the promises made to Israel.

Even among Dispensationalists, this causes some diversity of opinion within the pretribulational camp as Trahan notes:

> There is some disagreement among pretribulationalists as to whether the Old Testament saints will be included in the Rapture. While it is true that followers of Darby have generally interpreted the Rapture to include all saints, a very common alternative explanation is that *only* the Church, the saints of this present age, are raised at the Rapture, and that the Old Testament saints are raised at the occurrences described in Revelation 20:4.[184] In regards to this explanation, Walvoord comments as follows: "the fact is there is no Scriptural proof that the Old Testament saints are raised at the Rapture."[185] [186]

Perhaps here Dispensationalists make too much of the Israel/Church distinction as taught in the Bible. If the promises to Israel are large enough to include the Church, there is little problem having the Church and Israel in co-existence.

Therefore, to state that because the New Covenant of Jeremiah is made to the house of Israel and Judah, and

---

184 John F. Walvoord, "A Review of the Blessed Hope by George E. Ladd," *Bibliotheca Sacra* (Dallas, TX: Dallas Theological seminary, 1996). Quoted in Trahan, 209.

185 Ibid.

186 Trahan, 209.

therefore cannot apply to the Church is incorrect. Yes, at the time of revelation, making a promise to the Gentiles for salvation was somewhat hidden within God's revelation as promised to Israel. But to deny that the Church can now share in those covenant promises misses the entire point of why Christ came, to bring Jew and Gentile together in the Church. Regardless of what happens subsequent to the Church Age, the promises of the New Covenant are clearly made to the houses of Israel and Judah, but are currently being enjoyed in large part by the Gentiles. In the same way, the atoning sacrifice of Jesus Christ is the basis on which Old Testament saints find eternal life, but this does not make Old Testament saints part of the Church. So is the Church completely unknown and totally hidden in the Old Testament? The answer is yes only if one believes the Jeremiah passage is not for the Church and therefore has not begun, and no one would argue this. But in so including the Church with Israel does not mean that Israel and the Church are the same, even though in many ways they share similarities. Israel always refers to ethnic and national Israel in the Bible, without exception. But Israel, and even the term "All Israel" does not always include every Israelite. Context must be determinative.

The first instance of "All Israel" in the HCSB is in Exodus 18:24-26:

> 24 Moses listened to his father-in-law and did everything he said. 25 So Moses chose able men from all Israel and made them leaders over the people [as] officials of thousands, hundreds, fifties, and tens. 26 They judged the people at all times; the hard cases they would bring to Moses, but every minor case they would judge themselves.

Here "All Israel" does appear to include every single Israelite.

The next occurrence is Deuteronomy 1:1 when Moses speaks to "All Israel" across the Jordan. In Deuteronomy 5:1 Moses summons "All Israel" to him in order to recount the Law. He references "All Israel" again in Deuteronomy 13:11 and refers there to the entire nation. Deuteronomy 21:21 is a similar usage. The remaining references in Deuteronomy are likewise spoken to the entire nation (Deuteronomy 27:9; 29:1; 31:1,7,11(2x); 32:44; 34:12).

In Joshua the Lord speaks to Joshua and references "All Israel":

> The LORD spoke to Joshua: "Today I will begin to exalt you in the sight of all Israel, so they will know that I will be with you just as I was with Moses. 8 Command the priests carrying the ark of the covenant: 'When you reach the edge of the waters, stand in the Jordan.' "

Every instance thus far in reference to "All Israel" includes all of national Israel. In Joshua 3:17 when crossing the Jordan, again "All Israel" is mentioned in reference to every Israelite. The reference is to all again in Joshua 4:14 as it is in the stoning of Achan (Joshua 7:24,25).

The first reference to "All Israel" being a group comprised of less than every Israelite is in Joshua 8:15. During the conquest of the Land, the LORD told Joshua to take the military force and attack Ai (Joshua 8:1). Joshua chose 300,000 fighting men (8:3) and attacked Ai. The usage of "All Israel" in 8:15 and again in 8:21 and 8:24 is referring not to every single Israelite, but only those in the military conflict. Therefore "All Israel" is demonstrated to be used at least once for a group of Israelites that includes less than every single one.

The next reference to "All Israel" is located in Joshua 8:33 where "All Israel, foreigner and citizen alike, with their elders, officers, and judges, stood on either side of the ark of the Lord's covenant facing the Levitical priests who carried it." The reference to All Israel in this instance includes not only every national Israelite and includes foreigners who had become Jews as well.

The reference to "All Israel" is in Joshua 10:15 comes after the defeat of the Amorite kings. Similar to the attack on Ai, the reference here is to less than every Israelite and is specific to the military group which Joshua took with him to fight. This usage continues throughout the conquest (Joshua 10:29,31,34,36,38,43). The usage switches back to "all" meaning everyone in Joshua 23:2 as Joshua summons Israel together to review the history of Israel and renew the covenant.

The next instance of "All Israel" is in the Judges and will serve as the last example of how the term "All Israel" can sometimes refer to every national Israelite and at other times merely to a segment. In Judges 8:27 "all Israel" is said to have prostituted themselves to an idol. The colloquialism of "All Israel" does not mean each and every single Israelite participated in the idolatry, although this is possible, but the Israelites who did participate in the idolatry are who is in mind with the reference to "All Israel."

What this inquiry into the biblical uses of "All Israel" sets up is Paul's usage of the term in Romans 11 to discuss "All Israel" being saved. He is clearly speaking of national Israelites, for there is no other usage of such a term other than national Israelites in Scripture, and God does not intend for every Israelite to be saved. He knows too well many of his fellow Jews will not be included in "All Israel," but to say that Paul had in mind all the redeemed, both Jews and Gentiles while expounding upon God's promises to ethnic Israel, is not an acceptable reading of the text. What this does demonstrate is that God is not done with national Israel, and if He was, Paul spoke untruly in Romans 11. Paul makes it crystal clear that ethnic Israel is not out of God's plans, he states:

> So that you will not be conceited, brothers, I do not want you to be unaware of this mystery: a partial hardening has come to Israel until the full number of the Gentiles has come in. 26 And in this way all Israel will be saved, as it is written:
> **The Liberator will come from Zion;**
> **He will turn away godlessness from Jacob.**
> **27 And this will be My covenant with them,**
> **when I take away their sins.**
>
> 28 Regarding the gospel, they are enemies for your advantage, but regarding election, they are loved because of their forefathers, 29 since God's gracious gifts and calling are irrevocable. 30 As you once disobeyed God, but now have received mercy through their disobedience, 31 so they too have now disobeyed, [resulting] in mercy to you, so that they also now may receive mercy. 32 For God has imprisoned all in disobedience, so that He may have mercy on all (Romans 11:25-32).

What is one to make of this? Replacement Theology would understand this as the saved of all generations. The Church is now added to believers from the Old Testament to comprise "all Israel." If this approach is taken; however, verse 26 would read, "And in this way all "who are saved" will be saved." While not impossible, this is certainly an awkward reading and as stated above would make Paul at odds with God's plans for national Israel.

Covenantal Dispensationalists should understand this verse as they understand all references to the Church, Israel, salvation, and the elect; in light of the eternal promise of God to save and redeem that which was lost. The context of chapter 11 of Romans must be taken into account when determining who "all Israel" means in this specific verse. Paul is hopeful a day will come when ethnic Jews will flock to their messiah in droves.

As to the timing of this great turning of Israel to their Messiah this work now seeks to examine. The eschatological views will be discussed in the following chapter to see if any particular view would fit with this expanded understanding of Dispensationalism or if there is one view that must be held.

CHAPTER 13

OTHER IRRECONCILABLE DIFFERENCES

The limits of space prevent a detailed explanation for all of the differences that have sprung up between Covenant Theology and Dispensationalism, but a few stances on various issues that appear to be mutually exclusive will be considered in this chapter.[187] The format of this chapter will be a listing of some of the differences between Dispensationalism and Covenant Theology followed by brief commentary. An exhaustive list of differences is not included, but a few major differences will be discussed.

Dispensationalism: Most are Arminian, but many are Amyraldian (4-point Calvinist).

---

187 The chart used in this chapter is based on the differences compiled by Jason Robertson on his website, http://fide-o.com/2009/05/comparing-dispensational-theology-and-covenant-theology/ [accessed 12/30/2009].

Covenant Theology: Usually Calvinist.

As mentioned previously, Calvinism is not the exclusive property of Covenant Theology. There is nothing in the dispensational system as presented that would prevent someone from holding to all five points of Calvinism. It is true that most Dispensationalists are less Calvinistic than are Covenant theologians, but the reason is that Covenant Theology sprung up out of a Reformed basis, while Dispensationalism is generally not held by non-Reformed types.[188]

Dispensationalism: 'Israel' always means the literal, physical descendants of Jacob (ethnic Jews).

Covenant Theology: Depending on the context, 'Israel' may mean either physical descendents of Jacob, or "spiritual Israel" (who are people with faith in Christ like Abraham).

Israel, especially the term "All Israel" refers to the literal, physical descendants of Jacob. There are times, such as in Romans 11, where Israel does not refer to the entirety of the nation of Israel, but the Israel mentioned is clearly the redeemed, ethnic Jews. As mentioned earlier, the only passage that is somewhat debatable is Galatians 6:16, but as noted, *kai* in this verse should probably be understood as "even," thereby separating Israel from the Church. To spiritualize the term "Israel" is without warrant and changes the term into something the Bible never intended. Christians do not become Jews or Israelites upon conversion.

Dispensationalism: The Church was born at Pentecost after the Ascension of Christ.

---

188 An example of a 5-point Calvinist and a Dispensationalist is Dr. Stephen Carlson, Editor and Bible Translator.

> Covenant Theology: The Church began in the
> Garden of Eden and grew in the Old Testament
> with the Old Testament covenants and reached
> fulfillment in the New Testament with the New
> Covenant in Jesus Christ. God has one family, one
> Church, one flock, one baptism, one way of salvation
> whether before the Cross or after – by grace alone
> through faith alone in Christ alone.

The trap set here by Covenant theologians is the implicit accusation that Dispensationalism has more than one way of salvation, which is untrue. Also, God has one family is accepted by Dispensationalists if by the term it means the family is comprised of the redeemed. There were redeemed persons before Israel, during the Old Testament, and after the foundation of the Church. The next words, "one Church," are intended to be read by the student to mean that one family is equal to the one Church, but as Chapter 12 explains, the Church did not begin until Christ established it. To mix the Church with the redeemed of all time creates an anachronism in the Old Testament.

> Dispensationalism: God's laws as given in the Old
> Testament are no longer in effect unless repeated in
> the New Testament.

> Covenant Theology: God's moral laws are eternal
> and are thus in effect forever. Old Testament laws
> for the government of Israel and temple activity are
> no longer useful since the inauguration of the New
> Covenant.

This discrepancy is perhaps the most dense with misunderstanding of any studied. The idea that God's laws are no longer in effect unless repeated in the New Testament demonstrates a complete understanding of both how Dispensationalists view God's laws and the Law. God's law is written on man's heart, and there is no need for repetition on certain matters. Murder, for instance, was presented by God as unethical before the giving of the Law. There does not need to be a repeat of this for believers in the Age of Grace to know murder is wrong. Also, the Law is no longer in effect according to Hebrews, and there is no hint that only certain parts of the Law are no longer applicable, but the whole Law. Dispensationalists would heartily agree that God's moral laws are eternal and would agree that the Law is no longer for today. The listing under Covenant Theology could fit perfectly well under Dispensationalism, and the one for Dispensationalism is completely wrong-headed.

Dispensationalism: Most teach that men in the Old Testament were saved by faith in a revelation peculiar to their Dispensation.

Covenant Theology: All men who have ever been saved have been saved by faith in Christ as their sin-bearer, which has been progressively revealed in every age.

How this alleged discrepancy is anything other than semantic wordplay is untenable. Dispensationalists have faith in the revelation of God to the extent it has been revealed as do Covenant theologians. To state that Covenant Theology teaches salvation by faith in Christ before Christ was present on the earth creates several problems. Both sides believe that faith and trust in God was required for salvation, but to what extent and how that is manifested, neither side has a better answer.

> Dispensationalism: Old Testament believers were not 'in Christ,' nor part of the Body or Bride of Christ even now.

> Covenant Theology: Believers in all ages are all 'in Christ' and part of the Body and Bride of Christ now.

The dispensational view that Old Testament believers were not 'in Christ' would be misleading if the term 'in Christ' was not properly defined. If, by 'in Christ' one means that an Old Testament believer's salvation is based on the shed blood of Christ, and the deceased believer's soul is now with Christ in Paradise, than yes, Old Testament believers are 'in Christ.' But 'in Christ' as the Church, the Bride of Christ, this did not exist in the Old Testament, therefore Old Testament believers could not be members of the Church. As noted in Chapter 12, there is some disagreement whether Old Testament saints will be Raptured due to their not being a part of the Church, but if by 'in Christ' one means they are outside of God's elect, this just is not so. The full benefits of eternal life are for all men and women of faith in all ages.

This brief glance at some of the main differences between Dispensationalism and Covenant Theology has pointed out two things. First, as noted earlier, the defining of terms differently by different camps can often lead to misunderstandings. The same core belief may be held by both groups, but because of the way in which terms are used, terms such as "Church" or "People of God," the result is that one group believes the other holds to a different view than the one they truly possess. Secondly, there are some significant differences where it is necessary to simply point out that Covenant Theology is spiritualizing away clear teachings in Scripture that should be taken literally. One does not always need to take the Bible literally, but changing the meaning to suit a theological bent is not taking the Bible seriously.

CHAPTER 14

PREMILLENNIALISM REQUIRED

One additional subject that this work will address is that of the eschatological views that are related to Covenantal Dispensationalism. Eschatology is an area of wide disparity in views among evangelicals. The three basic views concerning the Millennium are Premillennialism, Amillennialism, and Postmillennialism. For the sake of space, the views on the Rapture will not be covered in this work.

Covenantal theologians have been involved with all three positions regarding Revelation 20, however, Dispensationalism is always associated with Premillennialism. To begin, a review of Amillennialism and Postmillennialism will be conducted.

Louis Berkhof (1873-1957), a stalwart in Reformed circles helps define Amillennialism:

The Amillennial view is, as the name indicates, purely negative. It holds that there is no sufficient Scriptural ground for the expectation of a Millennium, and is firmly convinced that the Bible favors the idea that the present dispensation of the Kingdom of God will be followed immediately by the Kingdom of God in its consummate and eternal form."[189]

While this work is unable to provide an exhaustive apologetic for Premillennialism, a word about the difficulties that exist concerning Amillennialism must be noted. Millard Erickson says of Premillennialism:

There are no biblical passages with which Premillennialism cannot cope, or which it cannot adequately explain. We have seen, on the other hand, that the reference to two resurrections (Rev. 20) gives Amillennialists difficulty. Their explanations that we have here two different types of resurrection or two spiritual resurrections strain the usual principles of hermeneutics. The Premillennialist case appears stronger at this point . . .

. . . Accordingly, we judge the Premillennial view to be more adequate than Amillennialism.[190]

By extension, Erickson's argument would be the same for Postmillennialism, a view covered below, because Postmillennialism suffers from the same two resurrection problem that Amillennialism faces.

One area of controversy that has only been briefly made mention of in the present work is the allegorical interpretive

---

189 Berkhof, 708.

190 Millard Erickson, *Christian Theology* (Grand Rapids, MI: Baker Academic, 2006), 1216-1217.

approach to the Bible that most Covenant theologians take. This approach to interpreting the Bible comes to the center state when explaining Amillennialism because of its allegorical, non-literal approach to Revelation 20.

Trahan explains that "the history of Amillennialism can be traced to the Church fathers, particularly to the allegorical interpretive approaches to the Scriptures of Origen and Clement of Alexandria. Augustine adopted and further developed this allegorical method of interpretation, especially applying it to interpretation of prophecy."[191]

Replacement Theology also plagues this view of the Millennium held by many Covenantal theologians. Lewis explains, "Covenant theologians generally think they are justified in interpreting all the promises to Israel as fulfilled in the Church, and often do not anticipate a historical Millennium."[192] Some Covenant theologians exist that would be Premillennial, but the majority do not agree with Premillennialism. Since the time of the Protestant Reformation, another view of the Millennium has emerged called Postmillennialism.

Postmillennialism is "actually a fairly recent system, having been formulated after the Protestant Reformation."[193] Charles Hodge, one of the leaders in Reformed thought during the nineteenth Century explains the other major view regarding the Millennium known as Postmillennialism:

> Before the second coming of Christ there will be a time of great and long continued prosperity to be followed by a season of decay and of suffering, so that when the Son of man comes, He shall hardly find faith on the earth . . This period is called a

---

191 Trahan, 201.

192 Gordon R. Lewis, "Theological Antecedents of Pretribulationalism," *Biblia Sacra* (Dallas, TX: Dallas Theological Seminary, 1996).

193 Karleen.

Millennium because in Revelation it is said to last a thousand years, an expression which is generally understood in a literal sense. Some, however, think it means a protracted season of indefinite duration, as when it is said that one day is with the Lord as a thousand years. . . . During this period, whatever its length, the Church is to enjoy a season of peace, purity, and blessedness such as it has never yet experienced."[194]

Even within Premillennialism, there are those who hold to the proper view of the Millennium, but not for the proper reasons. The reason Premillennialism is "required" is because it does justice to the thousand year reign of Christ being the fulfillment of all the promises made to Israel. Even so, the distinction between Israel and the Church should not be blurred, but with the new revelation of the New Testament, the promises to Israel have clearly been extended to the Church. The parasite that needs to be removed from Classical Premillennialism is the replacement aspect of the Church for Israel.

George Eldon Ladd is one such Covenantal Premillennialist, and he states that, "the Old Testament is reinterpreted in light of the Christ event."[195] He goes on to explain why the Church and Israel are merged together as one people of God. In light of Romans 9:24-26 he argues that, "Old Testament prophecies must be interpreted in the light of the New Testament to find their deeper meaning."[196] Unfortunately he makes the unwarranted conclusion that because believing Jews and the Church are all the people of

---

194 Hodge, *Systematic Theology*, 3:857-9.

195 George Eldon Ladd, *The Meaning of the Millennium* (Downers Grove, IL: InterVarsity Press, 1977), 21.

196 Ibid., 23.

God, then they must be the same. Therefore it is not surprising that he comes to a conclusion that makes no sense with the case he has built, "There are admittedly serious theological problems with the doctrine of a Millennium. However, even if theology cannot find an answer for all its questions, evangelical theology must build upon the clear teaching of Scripture. Therefore I am a Premillennialist."[197]

Ladd's conclusion is accurate; there will be a literal Millennium. But due to his wholesale rejection of Dispensationalism and the Israel-Church distinctions, he has evidence for a different conclusion from the one he expresses. Therefore, from a logical standpoint, Israel and the Church must be distinct at some level, if the Millennium is indeed purposed for a time of fulfillment to ethnic Israel. The most sensible reconciliation to this is that the Church and Israel are distinct. When Christ returns, He will raise the righteous dead and all those who are His will reign with Him for a thousand years. If Israel is absorbed into the Church, what purpose does the Millennium serve?[198]

This is not an isolated occurrence; most nondispensational Premillennialists come to similar or the exact same conclusion that the Millennium is unnecessary. The reason for this is

---

197 Ibid., 40.

198 Ladd suggests three reasons for the Millennium despite a replacement theological outlook in his book, *The Meaning of the Millennium*. Unfortunately, all three are mere conjecture and do not fit with the biblical record. He postulates that the (1) the Millennium is part of Christ's messianic rule by which he puts all his enemies under his feet (1 Cor 15:25); (2) So that Christ's Messianic kingdom might be disclosed in history and the "Age to Come will be beyond history so the Millennium will be used by God as a way of consummating the kingdom of His Son in history before all things change (page 39)"; and (3) the Millennium will serve to validate or commend the justice of God at the Great White Throne judgment. All three of these explanations fit perfectly well with the dispensational understanding of the Millennium (i.e. that Christ will rule in physical Jerusalem, that his kingdom shall come down to earth and validate his justice).

because they interpret the two resurrections of Revelation 20 correctly, but not the significant differences that exist between Israel and Church. Millard Erickson is but another example of this, believing the Millennium to be taught by Scripture, but serving no purpose.[199] These men come to the correct conclusion regarding the fact that a Millennium is taught in Scripture, but due to the lack of appreciation for the promises made to ethnic Israel that must be fulfilled, end up with a Millennium without a purpose.

Merrill makes clear the necessity for God to fulfill the promises made to Israel:

> Bible Scholars are virtually unanimous in their agreement that an exile of Israel did occur and that it was reversed by the return of the Jews to their homeland coincident with the decree of Cyrus in 538 B.C. There is no consensus, however, about whether or not the historical restoration completely fulfills the prophecies. But it is clear to me that the condition of the restored community and the mode and process of the return fell short of the extravagant prophecies. Therefore, the only way to harmonize the prophecies with the historical event is to find their fulfillment through the Church—the new Israel—or to posit an eschatological fulfillment in which a literal, physical Israel will be gathered to the land and assume her role as a redemptive community functioning culturally and politically in a manner akin to that of the ancient covenant nation.[200]

---

199 Erickson.

200 Eugene H. Merrill. "Pilgrimage and Procession: Motifs of Israel's Return," in *Israel's Apostasy and Restoration: Essays in Honor of Roland K. Harrison.* Edited by Avraham Gileadi. (Grand Rapids, Michigan: Baker Book House, 1988), 261-62.

and derived status of the Covenant of Redemption and even that of the Covenant of Grace make pinning down such minutiae difficult. But for the Covenantal theologian, there is no future covenant to be administered. So as for the future covenants to come, there is unanimity in the idea that there will be no further covenants. At God's appointed time, He will bring history to a close and usher in the Eternal State.

For Dispensationalism, the future is both clear and not so clear. Clearly the Millennial reign of Christ is subsequent to this present dispensation. In addition to this, a small number of Dispensationalists treat the tribulation and the Eternal State as dispensations, so the disagreement is not about what is to come, but how to label the periods still remaining in human history. All Dispensationalists would agree that mankind is currently in the economy or Dispensation of Grace, even if all would not use that term. Clarence Larkin, for instance, uses the title of "Ecclesiastical Dispensation."[201] Harold Wilmington refers to the present dispensation that spans, in his view, from the upper room to the Rapture, as the dispensation of the bride of the lamb.[202] Charles Ryrie's term for this present dispensation is that of the Gentiles.[203] Most other Dispensationalists use the aforementioned Dispensation of Grace, or perhaps that of the dispensation of the Church. Regardless of the terminology used, the dispensation is the same in character.

And all would agree that the Millennium will follow the present dispensation. The Eternal State, though mentioned as a dispensation by some, is agreed upon by Dispensationalists to take place after the dispensation which follows the present one. Whether or not the Eternal State gets the title

---

201 Clarence Larkin, *Dispensational Truth, or God's Plan and Purpose in the Ages* (New York: Cosimo, Inc., 2008, originally published 1918).

202 Wilmington, 821.

203 Ryrie.

of "dispensation" does not change the agreement as to the present and future arrangements between God and man that exist in dispensational though.

The present dispensation is characterized by the full revelation of Jesus Christ. The canon is closed and Christ has spoken through His words recorded in Scripture. Grace is offered to Jews and Gentiles. The Church stands and the gates of Hades have yet to, and will not, overcome it. The Law is no longer in effect, the gospel of Jesus Christ goes forth, and individuals are saved and join the community of faith in a local Church.

The Covenant of Grace, the Dispensation of Grace and the era of the promise are still in effect. They exist side by side and as long as people recognize Christ as the risen son of God, the Church will continue to grow. Even during the tribulation there will be those that come to faith. But there will be a tribulation, followed by a Millennial reign of Christ after His return, then followed by the Great White Throne or Final Judgment, and than the Eternal State where believers abide with God forever, and sin is no more.

CONCLUSION

The original hypothesis for this work was stated in the Introduction as: *Is Covenant Theology truly incompatible with the teachings of Dispensationalism? Could there be room at the "theological table" for a hybrid approach to these systems? Is Covenantal Dispensationalism a valid "new" hermeneutical school embracing the biblical aspects of both systems while rejecting the unbiblical aspects?* After surveying both Dispensationalism and Covenant Theology, the more adequate way of understanding the Bible is clearly Dispensationalism if one is compelled to choose between the two schools of interpretation. The idea that Covenant Theology is a legitimate and appropriate school of interpretation has been shown to be weak at best. Within Covenant Theology a lot of valid, biblical truths are present, but as a system of interpreting the Bible, the speculation and conjecture required and hermeneutical gymnastics are not profitable for a student of the Bible.

Perhaps the numerous changes that would be required of Covenant Theology to bring it into accordance with what the author believes to be the true teaching of Scripture would be too much for a Covenantal theologian to acquiesce to. The idea of "Covenantal Dispensationalism," therefore, does not appear to be an appropriate "new" hermeneutical school unless Covenant Theology was willing to concede on such points as a distinction between Israel and the Church, the discontinuity between the Law and the New Testament, non-Premillennial views of eschatology, and the unscriptural practice of infant baptism. However, both sides of the hermeneutical issue have a high view of Scripture, and certainly agree that whatever the Bible teaches is truth and should be followed, but there are some fundamental issues about what those teachings are that will undoubtedly lead both sides to a stalemate. Therefore, the conclusion is that Dispensationalism is a closer representation of the Bible's teaching, but the idea of a covenant or plan of redemption as a way of understanding unity throughout the entirety of Scripture is a welcome addition to a dispensational understanding of God's Word.

A quick summation of Covenantal Dispensationalism would be thus: it is best understood as the basic and general teachings of Dispensationalism, but with an eye to the overall Covenant of Redemption flowing through the various dispensations as found in the biblical record. One of the major sticking points is the Church/Israel distinction between the two schools. The Church is not a continuation of Israel. The promises made to Abraham were for anyone who would believe, and this included a time before there was a Church. The promises were also to national Israel. Old Testament believers are not "grandfathered" into the Church, but are included in Covenant Theology's Covenant of Grace along with everyone who comes to faith. However, according to the Covenant theologians studied, this does not appear to be a point at which Covenant Theology would agree. Additionally, infant baptism shows a very important misunderstanding of the covenant community concept. The sign of being a covenant member is always a circumcision of the heart, it is inward. In the New Testament an outward identification sign of membership is baptism, but it is reserved for believers. In this manner, Covenant Theology errs by being overly committed to continuity between the testaments, instead of understanding the temporary nature of the law and the differences that exist between Israel and the Church.

The mystery of the Church was also examined in this work. While perhaps not a complete parenthetical entity as Dispensationalism often declares, the Church was not present in the Old Testament. The mystery Paul speaks about has been shown to be the further revelation of Jesus Christ; that Jews and Gentiles can now be one body of Christ; that the Law has been abrogated by Christ; that any man or woman can be saved by placing his or her faith in Jesus Christ. The mystery is more than just the Church. The mystery unfolds the entire plan of God and has opened wider to encompass Gentiles who are no longer required to become Jews to be part of the chosen nation, the royal priesthood.

An additional finding of this study is that neither Covenant Theology nor Dispensationalism can adequately explain election prior to Christ, and Covenantal Dispensationalism would not be a helpful school for solving this dilemma. God elected whom He elected, for His own purposes, and the criterion remains in the secret counsel of God (Deut. 29:29). Various saved persons demonstrated this faith in various ways (Hebrews 11), but to point to a certain set of objective facts that would demonstrate knowledge of the gospel along with faith in God consistent throughout the Old Testament and applicable to persons before Christ is not possible. The main thing is faith in God and belief in Him was required based on the extent that God had revealed Himself to that point

While the end result after reading a persuasive paper may have mixed results, the author does not doubt that entrenched individuals of either camp will believe the arguments were not presented fairly, the true disagreements were not addressed, or will find some reason to treat Covenantal Dispensationalism in the same way Grape Nuts or Christian Science are treated, as neither covenantal or dispensational. Covenantal theologians might object to the a priori acceptance of believer's baptism as consistent with how Christ would have members of the new covenant make known their acceptance of the gospel, while Dispensationalists may find this presentation has too large of a focus on the Church *and* Israel rather than the Church *versus* Israel, but in the end, the purpose of this endeavor was not to simply point out the deficiencies in the theological system of Covenant Theology, nor was it to serve as an unapologetic apologetic for Dispensationalism. Also, the goal in and of itself was not to create a new position that presents itself as a hybrid hermeneutic between the two hermeneutical schools of Covenant Theology and Dispensationalism, but to see how closely each school of interpretation matches up to the biblical data. Does one need to become a Covenantal Dispensationalist to understand properly God's eternal plans regarding the destiny of ethnic Jews as well as the method upon which God chooses His elect for salvation? No. The point is that a broader understanding of God's interaction with His created beings is in order, and a fresh look at His dealings especially with the Jews and more broadly with each and every individual who has ever lived is indeed a worthy effort.

Hal Harless, who has addressed the same issue as the present work, comes to the following conclusions which are strikingly similar to arguably any serious study of the imbedded beliefs that adherents of either position would come to:

> What is required is a Covenantal Dispensationalism. Since Covenant Theology has commandeered the term 'covenant' many would consider 'dispensational Covenant Theology' or 'covenant Dispensationalism' oxymorons. Ultimately, these

distinctions stem from a false dichotomy. The Scriptures are both covenantal and dispensational. *Covenants prescribe and dispensations describe the structure of the progressive revelation of God's plan for the ages.* God's administration of humankind is founded upon the bedrock of His covenant promises[204]

Perhaps no simpler statement could be found apart from Harless' statement, "covenants prescribe and dispensations describe the structure of the progressive revelation of God's plan for the ages."[205] One should not claim to be a covenantalist if he or she is not also ready to admit that within the spectrum of time, as God's revelation was progressively revealed, He chose to place regulations, guidance, and obligations on His people that differed from one period of time to another without obscuring the one redemptive plan through Christ established before the foundation of the world and set into motion and achieved through multiple dispensations, but always applied to a believer by grace.

Likewise, the Dispensationalist should readily admit that the basis of salvation has been and always will be on the shed blood of Jesus Christ. But as to how this was understood before the crucifixion by God's people will remain somewhat of a mystery. The differences between Israel and the Church are real, but are both included in the New Covenant. The Church, if any such terminology be used, was grafted in, or the promises to Israel were extended to the Church. For where would a Jew who comes to faith turn, but to the Church, where all who believe in the Lord Jesus Christ should turn? After the advent of the Church, it has become

---

204 Hal Harless, *How Firm a Foundation: The Dispensations in Light of the Divine Covenants* (New York: Peter Lang Publishing, 2004), 279.

205 Ibid.

the home for Jews and Gentiles alike. No, what God has done is progressively administer His grace outwards, in an ever expanding way, to now encompass Jews and Gentiles. The Church is not an intercalation or a parenthesis in the plan God has for Israel, for Christ's death on the cross, His establishment of His Church, has always been the plan to extend the community of faith to those who were far off, even if this was not disclosed in the Old Testament.

One final caveat should be noted. Despite the best ecumenical efforts and acceptance of a wider range of meaning with theological terms (such as grace and dispensations), the present author believes the eschatological positions of Amillennialism and Postmillennialism do not hold up to exegetical scrutiny and should be rejected by Covenantalists and Dispensationalists alike; although within the Dispensational camp this is not asking a great deal. As to the timing of the Rapture in relation to the Second Coming of Christ, the author believes latitude exists among Premillennialists to have such a conversation, but that conversation is not an emphasis in this work and will be tabled for another time. The reason this same allowance for differences of thought is not extended to Millennial differences is due to the strong conviction of this author that the differences between the timing of the Rapture and the substance of the thousand year reign of Christ are qualitatively different arguments, neither of which will be discussed in this work.

If at the conclusion of a fair reading of the arguments presented and the conclusions reached, a reader can look at the Dallas Theological Seminary's statement concerning Covenant Theology and understand more clearly that the Covenant of Grace is not as tied to Dispensationalism as one may have first believed or if a Reformed Presbyterian , or similar covenantalist of any denominational affiliation, engages in doctrinal discussions with a Fundamental Baptist concerning Dispensationalism, he or she does not come to the discussion with the presupposition that the Baptist believes that there are multiple ways a person can get saved depending on when they lived, or even how Jews might now come to salvation in a way related to their covenant status as God's chosen people in lieu of faith in Christ, then the idea of Covenantal Dispensationalism has achieved its objective. Even if there is no one in the Church or in the classroom who would ever claim to be a Covenantal Dispensationalist, perhaps those who glean from the theological camps that which is good may now have a more biblical understanding of God's amazing grace and His eternal promise that was made before time began. The promise was decided upon by God and is made to His elect. The promises by God are irrevocable, despite even the elect's ability to keep His commands. These promises are between God has His redeemed; to those whose names are written in the Lamb's Book of Life; the Lamb who was slain before the foundation of the world.

BIBLIOGRAPHY

Allen, W. C. *A Critical and Exegetical Commentary on the Gospel According to Matthew.* Edinburgh: T&T Clark, 1907.

Allis, Oswald T. *Prophecy and the Church.* Philadelphia: Presbyterian and Reformed, 1945.

Barker, Kenneth, General Editor. *The Zondervan NASB Study Bible.* Grand Rapids, MI: Zondervan, 1999.

Barth, Karl. *Church Dogmatics.* New York: T&T Clark International, 1958.

Berkhof, Louis. *Systematic Theology.* Grand Rapids: Eerdmans, 1941.

Blaising, Craig and Bock, Darrell. *Progressive Dispensationalism.* Wheaton, IL: BridgePoint, 1993.

Bloomfield, S. T. *The Greek Testament with English Notes,* Vol. I. Boston: Perkins & Marvin, 1837.

Bradshaw, Robert I. "Covenant," http://www.biblicalstudies.org.uk/article_covenant.html, 1998 (accessed 12/10/2009).

Bromily, Geoffrey W. *Historical Theology: An Introduction.* Grand Rapids: Eerdmans, 1978.

Bruce, F. F. *The Canon of Scripture.* Downers Grove, IL: InterVarsity Press, 1988.

———. *New Testament History.* London: Doubleday, 1969.

_____ . *Israel and the Nations*. Carlisle: Paternoster Press, c1963, 1987.

Buswell, J. Oliver. *Systematic Theology of the Christian Religion*. Grand Rapids: Zondervan, 1962.

Carlson, Stephen W. "The Relevance of Apocalyptic Numerology for the Meaning of *XILIA ETH* in Revelation 20." Th.D. work, Mid-America Baptist Theological Seminary, 1990.

Carson, D. A. "Matthew," *The Expositor's Bible Commentary*, Volume 8. Frank Gaebelien, Ed., Grand Rapids: Zondervan, 1995.

Chafer, Lewis S. *Dispensationalism*. Dallas: Dallas Seminary Press, 1936.

_____ . *Systematic Theology*. Dallas, TX: Dallas Seminary Press, 1947.

"Charting Dispensationalism," *Christianity Today*. September 12, 1994.

Chisum, Berl. "Rightly Dividing the Word." http://www.Bibletruths.org/study/rightly.html (accessed 12/14/2009).

Clowney, Edmund P. *The Unfolding Mystery: Discovering Christ in the Old Testament*. Phillipsburgh, NJ: Presbyterian and Reformed, 1988.

Crutchfield, Larry. "Ages and Dispensations in the Ante-Nicene Fathers" *Bibliotheca Sacra*. October-December, 1987.

Dallas Theological Seminary, Doctrinal Statement. http://www.dts.edu/about/doctrinalstatement/ (accessed 09/23/2009).

Douglas, J. D., Comfort, P. W. & Mitchell, D., eds. *Who's Who in Christian History*. Wheaton, IL: Tyndale House, 1997.

Dumbrell, William J. *Covenant and Creation: A Theology of Old Testament Covenants*. Nashville: Thomas Nelson, 1984.

Duncan, J. Ligon. "What is Covenant Theology" http://www.fpcjackson.org/resources/apologetics/Covenant%20Theology%20&%20Justification/ligoncovt.htm (accessed 12/22/2009).

Easton, M. *Easton's Bible Dictionary*. Oak Harbor, WA: Logos Research Systems, Inc., 1996, c1897.

Elwell, W. A. & Beitzel, B. J. *Baker Encyclopedia of the Bible*. Grand Rapids, MI: Baker Book House, 1988.

Enns, Paul P. *The Moody Handbook of Theology*. Chicago: IL: Moody Press, 1997, c1989.

Erickson, Millard. *Christian Theology*. Grand Rapids, MI: Baker Academic, 2006.

Estep, William. *The Anabaptist Story*. Grand Rapids: Eerdmans, 1996.

Fackre, Gabriel J. *Ecumenical Faith in Evangelical Perspective*. Grand Rapids: Eerdmans, 1993.

Fahlbusch, E. & Bromiley, G. W. *The Encyclopedia of Christianity*. Grand Rapids: Eerdmans, 2003.

Feinberg, John S. ed. *Continuity and Discontinuity: Perspectives on the Relationship Between the Old and New Testaments.* Wheaton, IL: Crossway, 1988.

Gerstner, John H. *Wrongly Dividing the Word of Truth: A Critique of Dispensationalism.* Brentwood, TN: Wolgemuth & Hyatt, 1991.

Goldsworthy, Graeme, *According to Plan: The Unfolding Revelation of God in the Bible.* Downers Grove, IL: InterVarsity Press, 1991.

Harless, Hal. *How Firm a Foundation: The Dispensations in Light of the Divine Covenants.* New York: Peter Lang Publishing, 2004.

Heiron, George & Gary A.. "Covenant" David Noel Freedman, Editor-in-Chief, *Anchor Bible Dictionary,* Vol. 1. London: Doubleday, 1992.

Heppe, Heinrich. *Reformed Dogmatics.* Grand Rapids: Baker, 1978.

Hodge, Charles. *Systematic Theology.* Grand Rapids: Eerdmans, 1946.

Holy Bible, The: English standard version. Wheaton: Standard Bible Society, 2001.

Holy Bible, The : Holman Christian Standard Version. Nashville: Holman Bible Publishers, 2003.

Ice, Thomas. "A Short History of Dispensationalism." http://www.pre-trib.org/articles/view/short-history-of-Dispensationalism, (accessed 12/14/2009).

Jewett, Paul K. *Infant Baptism and the Covenant of Grace.* Grand Rapids: Eerdmans, 1980.

Karleen, Paul S. *The Handbook to Bible Study: With a Guide to the Scofield Study System.* New York: Oxford University Press, 1987.

Keil, C. F. and Delitzsch, F. "Minor Prophets," *Commentary on the Old Testament in Ten Volumes,* Vol. 10. Grand Rapids, MI: Eerdmans, 1988.

Kelly, Douglas et al., eds. *The Westminster Confession of Faith: A New Edition.* Greenwood, SC: Attic, 1981.

Ladd, George Eldon. *The Meaning of the Millennium.* Downers Grove, IL: InterVarsity Press, 1977.

Larkin, Clarence. *Dispensational Truth, or God's Plan and Purpose in the Ages.* New York: Cosimo, Inc., 2008, originally published 1918.

Lewis, Gordon R. "Theological Antecedents of Pretribulationalism," *Biblia Sacra.* Dallas, TX: Dallas Theological Seminary, 1996.

Longenecker, Richard. "Galatians," *Word Biblical Commentary,* Volume 41. Waco, TX: Word, 1990.

Luther, Martin. "On the Jews and Their Lies," in "Three Categories of Supersessionism" by Michael J. Vlach, http://www.theologicalstudies.org/page/page/1572335.htm (accessed December 22, 2009).

Mason, Clarence E. "A Review of Dispensationalism by John Wick Bowman: Part I," *Bibliotheca Sacra.* Dallas, TX: Dallas Theological Seminary, 1996, c1955-1995.

Merrill, Eugene H. "Pilgrimage and Procession: Motifs of Israel's Return," in *Israel's Apostasy and Restoration: Essays in Honor of Roland K. Harrison.* Edited by Avraham Gileadi. Grand Rapids, Michigan: Baker Book House, 1988.

Mills, M. *The Life of Christ: A study guide to the Gospel record.* Dallas, TX: 3E Ministries, 1999.

Newman, C. C. "Covenant, New Covenant," Ralph P. Martin & Peter H. Davids, *Dictionary of the Later New Testament.* Leicester: InterVarsity Press, 1997.

Nicholson, Ernest. *God and His People: Covenant and Theology in the Old Testament.* Oxford: Clarendon Press, 1998.

Osterhaven, M. E. "Covenant Theology" in Walter A. Elwell, ed., *Evangelical Dictionary of Theology.* Grand Rapids: Baker, 1984.

Owen, John. *The Works of John Owen,* Volume 12. London: Banner of Truth Trust, 1966.

Payne, J. Barton. *The Theology of the Older Testament.* Grand Rapids: Zondervan, 1962.

Pink, Arthur. *A Study in Dispensationalism.* http://www.pbministries.org/books/pink/Dispensationalism/Dispensationalism.htm. (accessed 11/12/2009).

Poythress, Vern S. *Understanding Dispensationalists,* 2nd ed. Phillipsburg, NJ: Presbyterian & Reformed, 1994.

Reisinger, Ernest. "A History of Dispensationalism in America," *The Founders Journal.* January/February 2009.

Robertson, Jason. http://fide-o.com/2009/05/comparing-dispensational-theology-and-covenant-theology/ (accessed 12/30/2009).

Robertson, O. Palmer. *The Christ of the Covenants.* Phillipsburgh, NJ: Presbyterian and Reformed, 1981.

Ryrie, Charles. *Dispensationalism.* Chicago: Moody Publishers, 2007.

Schaff, Philip. *The Creeds of Christendom with a History and Critical Notes, 3 Volumes.* Grand Rapids: Baker, 1977.

Scofield, C. I. *Rightly Dividing the Word of Truth.* http://www.biblebelievers.com/scofield/scofield_rightly02.html (accessed 12/30/2009).

Shedd, W. G. T. & Gomes, A. W. *Dogmatic Theology.* Phillipsburg, NJ: Presbyterian and Reformed, 2003.

Smith, J. E. *The Pentateuch.* Joplin, MO: College Press Pub. Co., 1993.

Strong, A. H. *Systematic Theology.* Bellingham, WA: Logos Research Systems, Inc., 2004.

Strong, J. *The exhaustive concordance of the Bible : Showing every word of the text of the common English version of the canonical books, and every occurrence of each word in regular order.* (electronic ed.) (G3807). Ontario: Woodside Bible Fellowship, 1996.

Stuart, Douglas. "Hosea-Jonah," *Word Biblical Commentary,* Vol. 31. Waco, TX: Word, 1987.

Tidwell, J. B. *The Bible Book by Book: A Manual for the Outline Study of the Bible by Books*. Waco, TX: Baylor University Press, 1916.

Trahan, Kerry. *A Complete Guide to Understanding the Dispensationalism Controversy*. Port Neches, TX: Disciple of Jesus Ministries, Inc., 2007.

Vincent, M. R. *Word Studies in the New Testament*. Bellingham, WA: Logos Research Systems, Inc., 2002.

Walvoord, John F. "A Review of the Blessed Hope by George E. Ladd," *Bibliotheca Sacra*. Dallas, TX: Dallas Theological seminary, 1996.

_____ . "Does the Church Fulfill Israel's Program? – Part 1," *Bibliotheca Sacra*. Dallas, TX: Dallas Theological Seminary, 1996.

Wenham, Gordon J. "The Book of Leviticus," *The New International Commentary on the Old Testament*. Grand Rapids: Eerdmans, 1979.

Wiersbe, W. W. *The Bible Exposition Commentary*. Wheaton, IL: Victor Books, 1996.

Wilder, Terry L., Charles, Daryl, & Easley, Kendell. *Faithful to the End: An Introduction to Hebrews through Revelation*. Nashville, TN: Broadman and Holman Publishing, 2007.

Wilmington, Harold. *Wilmington's Bible Handbook*. Wheaton, IL: Tyndale House Publishers, 1997.

Wright, N. T. *The New Testament and the People of God*. Minneapolis: Fortress, 1992.

_____. *Jesus and the Victory of God*. Minneapolis: Fortress, 1996.

Youngblood, Ronald. "The Abrahamic Covenant: Conditional or Unconditional?" in Morris Inch & Ronald Youngblood, eds. *The Living and Active Word of God*. Winona Lake, IN: Eisenbrauns, 1983.

Zuck, R. B. *A Biblical Theology of the New Testament*. Chicago: Moody Press, 1996.

PERSONAL PROFILE

Matthew Stamper is a continuous student of the Bible. As of the date of this publication, he continues to pursue degrees at the Southern Baptist Theological Seminary in Louisville, KY and at Union University in Jackson, TN. He holds a CPA license from the state of Tennessee and has worked in accounting and taxation for over ten years.

Matthew's church involvement involves short term missions, teaching Sunday School and leading Bible Study. He is a member of Central Baptist Church, a small congregation in Hendersonville, TN. He holds a Bachelor of Business Administration in Accounting as well as a Master of Accountancy from Belmont University in Nashville, TN. He is also a Ph.D. candidate in Biblical Studies at Louisiana Baptist University.

Matthew enjoys writing as well as teaching. He is an adjunct professor at Volunteer State Community College in Gallatin, TN. He also has a passion for baseball, especially the Los Angeles Angels of Anaheim. Matthew resides with his wife Maggie and two children, Taylor and MacKenzie, in the town where he was raised and currently serves the Lord, Hendersonville, TN.

Matthew is an ecumenical at heart and as a Southern Baptist seeks to reach out to groups who are often at odds theologically with one another as he demonstrates in this work. His favorite verse and the one that unites all believers is Romans 10:9, "if you confess with your mouth, 'Jesus is Lord,' and believe in your heart that God raised him from the dead, you will be saved." (NIV)